Autographs for Freedom.

AUTOGRAPHS

FOR FREEDOM.

EDITED BY

JULIA GRIFFITHS.

"In the long vista of the years to roll,
Let me not see my country's honor fade;
Oh! let me see our land retain its soul!
Her pride in Freedom, and not Freedom's shade."

AUBURN:
ALDEN, BEARDSLEY & CO.
ROCHESTER:
WANZER, BEARDSLEY & CO.

1854.

STEREOTYPED BY
THOMAS B. SMITH,
216 William St. N. Y.

Preface.

IN commending this, the second volume of "*the Autographs for Freedom*," to the attention of the public, "THE ROCHESTER LADIES' ANTI-SLAVERY SOCIETY" would congratulate themselves and the friends of freedom generally on the progress made, during the past year, by the cause to which the book is devoted.

We greet thankfully those who have contributed of the wealth of their genius; the strength of their convictions; the ripeness of their judgment; their earnestness of purpose; their generous sympathies; to the completeness and excellence of the work; and we shall hope to meet many of them, if not all, in other numbers of "*The Autograph*," which may be called forth ere the chains of the Slave shall be broken, and this country redeemed from the sin and the curse of Slavery.

On behalf of the Rochester Ladies' Anti-Slavery Society.

Julia Griffiths
Sec'y.

ROCHESTER, N. Y.,

Contents.

INTRODUCTION.

The Colored People's "Industrial College."

WHAT SOME OF THE BUILDERS HAVE THOUGHT.

A WORD oft-times is expressive of an entire policy. Such is the term *Abolition.* Though formerly used as a synonym of *Anti-Slavery*, people now clearly understand that the designs of those who have ranged themselves under the first of these systems of reform are of deeper significance and wider scope than are the objects contemplated by the latter, and concern themselves not only with the great primary question of bodily freedom, but take in also the collateral issues connected with human enfranchisement, independent of race, complexion, or sex.

The Abolitionist of to-day is the Iconoclast of the age, and his mission is to break the idolatrous images set up by a hypocritical Church, a Sham Democracy, or a corrupt public sentiment, and to substitute in their stead the simple and beautiful doctrine of a common brotherhood. He would elevate every creature by abolishing the hinderances and checks imposed upon him, whether these be legal or social—and in proportion as such grievances are invidious and severe, in such measure does he place himself in the front rank of the battle, to wage his emancipating war.

Therefore it is that the Abolitionist has come to be considered the especial friend of the negro, since *he*, of all others, has been made to drink deep from the cup of oppression.

The free-colored man at the north, for his bond-brother as for himself, has trusted hopefully in the increasing public sentiment, which, in the multiplication of these friends, has made his future prospects brighter. And, to-day, while he is making a noble struggle to vindicate the claims of his entire class, depending mainly for the accomplishment of that end on his own exertions, he passes in review the devotion and sacrifices made in his behalf: gratitude is in his heart, and thanks fall from his lips. But, in one department of reformatory exertion he feels that he has been neglected. He has seen his pledged allies throw themselves into the hottest of the battle, to fight for the Abolition of Capital Punishment—for the Prohibition of the Liquor Traffic—for the Rights of Women, and similar reforms,—but he has failed to see a corresponding earnestness, according to the influence of Abolitionists in the business world, in opening the avenues of industrial labor to the proscribed youth of the land. This work, therefore, is evidently left for himself to do. And he has laid his powers to the task. The record of his conclusions was given at Rochester, in July, and has become already a part of history.

Though shut out from the workshops of the country, he is determined to make self-provision, so as to triumph over the spirit of caste that would keep him degraded. The utility of the Industrial Institution he would erect, must, he believes, commend itself to Abolitionists. But not only to them. The verdict of less liberal minds has been given already in its favor. The usefulness, the self-respect and self-dependence,—the combination of intelligence and handicraft,—the accumulation of the materials of wealth, all referable to such an Institution, present fair claims to the assistance of the entire American people.

Whenever emancipation shall take place, immediate though it be, the subjects of it, like many who now make up the so-called free population, will be in what Geologists call, the "Transition State." The prejudice now felt against them for bearing on their persons the brand of slaves, cannot die out immediately. Severe trials will still be their portion—the curse of a "taunted race" must be expiated by almost miraculous proofs of advancement; and some of these miracles must be antecedent to the great day of Jubilee. To fight the battle on the bare ground of abstract principles, will fail to give us complete victory. The subterfuges of pro-slavery selfishness must *now* be dragged to light, and the last weak argument, —that the negro can never contribute anything to advance the national character, "nailed to the counter as base coin." To the conquering of the difficulties heaped up in the path of his industry, the free-colored man of the North has pledged himself. Already he sees, springing into growth, from out his foster *work-school*, intelligent young laborers, competent to enrich the world with necessary products—industrious citizens, contributing their proportion to aid on the advancing civilization of the country;—self-providing artizans vindicating their people from the never-ceasing charge of a fitness for servile positions.

Abolitionists ought to consider it a legitimate part of their great work, to aid in such an enterprise—to abolish not only chattel servitude, but that other kind of slavery, which, for generation after generation, dooms an oppressed people to a condition of dependence and pauperism. Such an Institution would be a shining mark, in even this enlightened age; and every man and woman, equipped by its discipline to do good battle in the arena of active life, would be, next to the emancipated bondman, the most desirable "*Autograph for Freedom.*"

Chas. L. Reason.

Massacre at Blount's Fort.

ON the west side of the Appalachicola River, some forty miles below the line of Georgia, are yet found the ruins of what was once called "BLOUNT'S FORT." Its ramparts are now covered with a dense growth of underbrush and small trees. You may yet trace out its bastions, curtains, and magazine. At this time the country adjacent presents the appearance of an unbroken wilderness, and the whole scene is one of gloomy solitude, associated as it is with one of the most cruel massacres which ever disgraced the American arms.

The fort had originally been erected by civilized troops, and, when abandoned by its occupants at the close of the war, in 1815, it was taken possession of by the refugees from Georgia. But little is yet known of that persecuted people; their history can only be found in the national archives at Washington. They had been held as slaves in the State referred to; but during the Revolution they caught the spirit of liberty, at that time so prevalent throughout our land, and fled from their oppressors and found an asylum among the aborigines living in Florida.

During forty years they had effectually eluded, or resisted, all attempts to re-enslave them. They were true to themselves, to the instinctive love of liberty, which is planted in every human heart. Most of them had been born amidst perils, reared in the forest, and taught from their childhood to hate the oppressors of their race. Most of those who had been personally held in degrading servitude, whose backs had been seared by the lash of the savage overseer, had passed to that spirit-land where the clanking of chains is not heard, where slavery is not known. Some few of that class yet remained. Their gray hairs and feeble limbs, however, indicated that they, too, must soon pass away. Of the three hundred and eleven persons residing in "Blount's Fort" not more than twenty had been actually held in servitude. The others were descended from slave parents, who fled from Georgia, and, according to the laws of slave

States, were liable to suffer the same outrages to which their ancestors had been subjected.

It is a most singular feature in slave-holding morals, that if the parents be robbed of their liberty, deprived of the rights with which their Creator has endowed them, the perpetrator of these wrongs becomes entitled to repeat them upon the children of their former victims. There were also some few parents and grandchildren, as well as middle-aged persons, who sought protection within the walls of the Fort against the vigilant slave-catchers who occasionally were seen prowling around the fortifications, but who dare not venture within the power of those whom they sought to enslave.

These fugitives had planted their gardens, and some of them had flocks roaming in the wilderness; all were enjoying the fruits of their labor, and congratulating themselves upon being safe from the attacks of those who enslave mankind. But the spirit of oppression is inexorable. The slaveholders finding they could not themselves obtain possession of their intended victims, called on the President of the United States for assistance to perpetrate the crime of enslaving their fellow men. That functionary had been reared amid southern institutions. He entertained no doubt of the right of one man to enslave another. He did not doubt that if a man held in servitude should attempt to escape, he would be worthy of death. In short, he fully sympathised with those who sought his official aid. He immediately directed the Secretary of War to issue orders to the Commander of the "Southern Military District of the United States" to send a detachment of troops to destroy "Blount's Fort," and to "*seize those who occupied it and return them to their masters.*"*

General Jackson, at that time Commander of the Southern Military District, directed Lieut.-Colonel Clinch to perform the barbarous task. I was at one time personally acquainted with that officer, and know the impulses of his generous nature, and can readily account for the failure of his expedition. He marched to the vicinity of the Fort, made the necessary recognisance, and returned, making report that "the fortification was not accessible by land."†

* Vide Executive documents of the 2d Session 13th Congress.

† It is believed that this report was suggested by the humanity of Col. Clinch. He was reputed one of the bravest and most energetic officers in the service. He possessed an indomitable perseverance, and could probably have captured the Fort in one hour, had he desired to do so.

Orders were then issued to Commodore Patterson, directing him to carry out the directions of the Secretary of War. He at that time commanded the American flotilla lying in "Mobile Bay," and instantly issued an order to Lieut. Loomis to ascend the Appalachicola River with two gun-boats, "to seize the people in BLOUNT'S FORT, deliver them to their owners, and destroy the Fort."

On the morning of the 17th Sept., A. D. 1816, a spectator might have seen several individuals standing upon the walls of that fortress watching with intense interest the approach of two small vessels that were slowly ascending the river, under full-spread canvas, by the aid of a light southern breeze. They were in sight at early dawn, but it was ten o'clock when they furled their sails and cast anchor opposite the Fort, and some four or five hundred yards distant from it.

A boat was lowered, and soon a midshipman and twelve men were observed making for the shore. They were met at the water's edge by some half dozen of the principal men in the Fort, and their errand demanded.

The young officer told them he was sent to make

demand of the Fort, and that its inmates were to be given up to the "slaveholders, then on board the gun-boat, who claimed them as fugitive slaves!" The demand was instantly rejected, and the midshipman and his men returned to the gun-boats and informed Lieut. Loomis of the answer he had received.

As the colored men entered the Fort they related to their companions the demand that had been made. Great was the consternation manifested by the females, and even a portion of the sterner sex appeared to be distressed at their situation. This was observed by an old patriarch, who had drunk the bitter cup of servitude, one who bore on his person the visible marks of the thong, as well as the brand of his master, upon his shoulder. He saw his friends faultered, and he spoke cheerfully to them. He assured them that they were safe from the cannon shot of the enemy—that there were not men enough on board the vessels to storm their Fort, and finally closed with the emphatic declaration: "*Give me liberty or give me death!*" This saying was repeated by many agonized fathers and mothers on that bloody day.

A cannonade was soon commenced upon the Fort, but without much apparent effect. The shots were harmless; they penetrated the earth of which the walls were composed, and were there buried, without further injury. Some two hours were thus spent without injuring any person in the Fort. They then commenced throwing bombs. The bursting of these shells had more effect. There was no shelter from these fatal messages. Mothers gathered their little ones around them and pressed their babes more closely to their bosoms, as one explosion after another warned them of their imminent danger. By these explosions some were occasionally wounded and a few killed, until, at length, the shrieks of the wounded and groans of the dying were heard in various parts of the fortress.

Do you ask why these mothers and children were thus butchered in cold blood? I answer, they were slain for adhering to the doctrine that "all men are endowed by their Creator with the *inalienable right to enjoy life and liberty*." Holding to this doctrine of Hancock and of Jefferson, the power of the nation was arrayed against them, and our army employed to deprive them of life.

The bombardment was continued some hours with but little effect, so far as the assailants could discover.

They manifested no disposition to surrender. The day was passing away. Lieut. Loomis called a council of officers and put to them the question, *what further shall be done?* An under officer suggested the propriety of firing "hot shot at the magazine." The proposition was agreed to. The furnaces were heated, balls were prepared, and the cannonade was resumed. The occupants of the Fort felt relieved by the change. They could hear the deep humming sound of the cannon balls, to which they had become accustomed in the early part of the day, and some made themselves merry at the supposed folly of their assailants. They knew not that the shot was heated, and was therefore unconscious of the danger which threatened them.

The sun was rapidly descending in the west. The tall pines and spruce threw their shadows over the fortification. The roar of the cannon, the sighing of the shot, the groans of the wounded, the dark shades of approaching evening, all conspired to render the scene one of intense gloom. They longed for the approaching night to close around them in order that they might bury the dead, and flee to the wilderness for safety.

Suddenly a startling phenomena presented itself to their astonished view. The heavy embankment and timbers protecting the magazine appeared to rise from the earth, and the next *instant* the dreadful explosion overwhelmed them, and the next found two *hundred and seventy* parents and children in the immediate presence of a holy God, making their appeal for retributive justice upon the government who had murdered them, and the freemen of the north who sustained such unutterable crimes.*

Many were crushed by the falling earth and the timbers; many were entirely buried in the ruins. Some were horribly mangled by the fragments of timber and the explosion of charged shells that were in the magazine. Limbs were torn from the bodies to which they had been attached. Mothers and babes lay beside each other, wrapped in that sleep which knows no waking.

The sun had set, and the twilight of evening was closing around them, when some sixty sailors, under the officer second in command, landed, and, without opposition, entered the Fort. The veteran sailors, accustomed to blood and carnage, were horror-stricken as they viewed the scene before them. They were accompanied, however, by some twenty slaveholders,

* That is the number officially reported by the officer in command, vide Executive doc. of the 13th Congress.

all anxious for their prey. These paid little attention to the dead and dying, but anxiously seized upon the living, and, fastening the fetters upon their limbs, hurried them from the Fort, and instantly commenced their return towards the frontier of Georgia. Some fifteen persons in the Fort survived the terrible explosion, and they now sleep in servile graves, or moan and weep in bondage.

The officer in command of the party, with his men, returned to the boats as soon as the slaveholders were fairly in possession of their victims. The sailors appeared gloomy and thoughtful as they returned to their vessels. The anchors were weighed, the sails unfurled, and both vessels hurried from the scene of butchery as rapidly as they were able. After the officers had retired to their cabins, the rough-featured sailors gathered before the mast, and loud and bitter were the curses they uttered against slavery and against those officers of government who had then constrained them to murder women and helpless children, merely for their love of liberty.

But the dead remained unburied; and the next day the vultures were feeding upon the carcasses of young men and young women, whose hearts on the previous morning had beaten high with expectation. Their bones have been bleaching in the sun for thirty-seven years, and may yet be seen scattered among the ruins of that ancient fortification.

Twenty-two years elapsed, and a representative in Congress, from one of the free States, reported a bill giving to the perpetrators of these murders a gratuity of five thousand dollars from the public treasury, as a token of the gratitude which the people of this nation felt for the soldierly and gallant manner in which the crime was committed toward them. The bill passed both houses of Congress, was approved by the President, and now stands upon our statute book among the laws enacted at the 3d Session of the 25th Congress.

The facts are all found scattered among the various public documents which repose in the alcoves of our National Library. But no historian has been willing to collect and publish them, in consequence of the deep disgrace which they reflect upon the American arms, and upon those who then controlled the government.

J R Giddings

The Fugitive Slave Act.

FEW laws have ever been passed better calculated than this to harden the heart and benumb the conscience of every man who assists in its execution. It pours contempt upon the dictates of justice and humanity. It levels in the dust the barriers erected by the common law for the protection of personal liberty. Its victims are native born Americans, uncharged with crime. These men are seized, without notice, and instantly carried before an officer, by whom they are generally hurried off into a cruel bondage, for the remainder of their days, and sometimes without time being allowed for a parting interview with their families. Such treatment would be cruel toward criminals; but these men are adjudged to toil, to stripes, to ignorance, to poverty, to hopeless degradation, on the pretence that they "owe service." This allegation all know to be utterly false, they having never promised to serve, and being legally incapable of making any contract. Every act of Christian kindness to these unhappy people, tending to secure to them the rights which our declaration of independence asserts belong *to all* men, is made by this accursed law a penal offence, to be punished with fine and imprisonment. Mock judges, unknown to the constitution, and bribed by the promise of double fees to re-enslave the fugitive, are commanded to decide, *summarily*, the most momentous personal issue, with the single exception of life and death, that could possibly engage the attention of a legal tribunal of the most august character. Yet this tremendous issue of liberty or bondage, is to be decided, not only in a hurry, but on such *prima facie* evidence as may satisfy the judge, and this judge, too, *selected* from a herd of similar creatures, by the claimant himself!! An *ex parte* affidavit, made by an absent and interested party, with the certificate of an absent judge that he believes it to be true, is to be received as CONCLUSIVE, in the face of any amount of oral and documentary testimony to the contrary. "Can a man take fire into his bosom and not be burned?" Can a man aid in executing such a law without defiling his own conscience? Yet does this profligate statute, with impious arrogance, command "ALL GOOD CITIZENS" to assist in enforcing it, when required so to do by an official slave-catcher!

It is a singular fact, in the history of this enactment, that Mr. Mason, who introduced the bill, and Mr. Webster, who, in advance, pledged to it his support "to the fullest extent," both confessed, on the floor of Congress, that in their individual judgments, it was UNCONSTITUTIONAL,—that is, that the constitution, as they expounded it, imposed upon the *States* severally, the obligation to surrender fugitive slaves, and gave Congress no power to legislate on the subject. The Supreme Court, however, having otherwise determined, these gentlemen acquiesced in its decision, without being convinced by it. It is well known how grossly Mr. Webster, in his subsequent canvass for the Presidency, insulted all who, like himself, denied the constitutionality of the law. Another significant fact in the same history is, that the law was passed by a *minority* of the House of Representatives. Of 232 members, only 109 recorded their names in its favor. Many, deterred either by scruples of conscience or doubts of the popularity of the measure, declined voting, while party discipline prevented them from offering to it an open and manly resistance. A third fact in this history, worthy to be remembered, is, that the advocates of the law are conscious that its revolting provisions would not bear discussion, forced its passage under the previous question, thus preventing any remarks on its enormities—any appeals to the consciences of the members—against the perpetration of such detestable wickedness.

Seldom has any public iniquity been committed to which the words of the Psalmist have been so applicable: "Surely the wrath of man shall praise THEE; and the remainder of wrath shalt THOU restrain."

It was happily so ordered, that several of the early seizures and surrenders under this law were conducted with such marked barbarity, such cruel indecent haste, such wanton disregard of justice and of humanity, as to shock the moral sense of the community, and to render the law intensely hateful.

Very soon after the law went into operation, one of the pseudo judges created by it, surrendered an alleged slave, on evidence which no jury would have deemed sufficient to establish a title to a dog. In vain the wretched man declared his freedom—in vain he named six witnesses whom he swore could prove his freedom—in vain he implored for a delay of ONE HOUR. He was sent off as a slave, guarded, at the expense of the United States treasury, to his pretended master in Maryland, who honestly refused to receive him. The judge had made a mistake (!) and had sent a free man instead of a slave.

This vile law, although of course receiving the sanction of the Democrats, it being a bid for the Presidency, was a device of the Whig party, and could not have been carried but by the co-operation of Webster, Clay, and Fillmore. As if to enhance the value of the bid, the Administration affected a desire to baptise it in northern blood, by making resistance to the law, a crime to be punished with DEATH. The hustling of an officer, and the consequent escape of an arrested fugitive, were declared, by the Secretary of State, to be a *levying of war against the United States*—of course an act of HIGH TREASON, to be expiated on the gallows; and the rioters at Christiana were prosecuted for HIGH TREASON, in pursuance of orders forwarded from Washington. This wretched sycophancy won no favor from the slaveholders, and the result of the abominable and absurd prosecution only brought on the authors and advocates of the law fresh obloquy. When men obtain some rich and splendid prize, by their wrong-doing, many admire their boldness and dexterity, but foolish, profitless wickedness ensures only contempt. The northern Whigs, in doing obeisance to the slave power, sinned against their oft-repeated and solemn professions and pledges. They sinned in the expectation of thereby electing a President, and enjoying the patronage he would dispense. Most bitterly were these men disappointed, first in the candidate selected, and next in the result of the election. The party has been beaten to death, and it died unhonored and unwept. Let the Fugitive Slave Law be its epitaph. Truly the Whig politicians were "snared in the work of their own hands."

Certain fashionable Divines deemed it expedient to second the efforts of the politicians in catching slaves, by talking from their pulpits about Hebrew slavery, and the reverence due to the "powers that be ordained of God." Yet the injunctions of the fugitive law were so obviously at variance with the "HIGHER LAW" of justice and mercy which these gentlemen were required by their Divine Master to inculcate, that "cotton divinity" fell into disrepute, nor could the plaudits of politicians and union committees save its clerical professors from forfeiting the esteem and confidence of multitudes of Christian people.

But Whig politicians and cotton Divines are not the only friends of the fugitive law to whom it has made most ungrateful returns. The Democratic leaders, bidding against the Whigs for the Presidency, were most vociferous in expressions of the delight they took in the human chase. Democratic candidates for the Presidency, to the goodly number of NINE, gave public attestations under their *signs manual*, of their approbation of a law outraging the principles of Democracy, as well as of common justice and humanity. Each and all of these men were rejected, and the slaveholders selected an individual whom they were well assured would be their obsequious tool, but who had offered no bribe for their votes.

But did the slaveholders themselves gain more by this law than their northern auxiliaries? They, indeed, hailed its passage as a mighty triumph. The nation had given them a law, drafted by themselves, laying down the rules of the hunt, as best suited their pleasure and interest. Wealthy and influential gentlemen in our commercial cities, out of compliment to southern electors, became amateur huntsmen, and in New York and Boston the chase was pursued with all the zeal and apparent delight that could have been expected in Guinea or Virginia. Slave-catching was the test, at once, of patriotism and gentility, while sympathy for the wretched fugitive was the mark of vulgar fanaticism. The north was humbled in the dust, by the action of her own recreant sons. Every "good citizen" found himself, for the first time in the history of mankind, a slave-catcher by law. Every official, appointed by a slave-catching judge, was invested with the authority of a High Sheriff, being empowered to call out the *posse comitatus*, and compel the neighbors to join in a slave chase. Well, indeed, might the slaveholders rejoice and make merry;—well, indeed, in the insolence of triumph, might they command the people of the north to hold their tongues about "the peculiar institution," under pain of their sore displeasure.

But amid this slavery jubilee, a woman's heart was swelling and heaving with indignant sorrow at the outrages offered to God and man by the fugitive law. Her pent up emotions struggled for utterance, and at last, as if moved by some mighty inspiration, and in all the fervor of Christian love, she put forth a book which arrested the attention of the WORLD. A miracle of authorship, this book attained, within twelve months, a circulation without a parallel in the history of printing. In that brief space, about two millions of volumes proclaimed, in the languages of civilization, the wrongs of the slave and the atrocities of the AMERICAN FUGITIVE LAW. The gaze of mankind is now turned upon the slaveholders and their northern auxiliaries, both clerical and lay. The subjects of European despotisms console themselves with the grateful conviction, that however harsh may be their own governments, they make no approach to the baseness or to the cruelty and tyranny of the "peculiar institution" of the Model Republic.*

* A late American traveller, in Germany, invited to an evening party at the house of a Professor, attempted to compliment the company by expressing his indignation at the oppression which "the dear old German fatherland" suffered at the hands of its rulers. The American's profferred sympathy was coldly received. "We admit," was the reply, "that there is much wrong here, but we do not admit the right of *your country* to rebuke it. There is a system now with you, worse than anything which we know of tyranny—your SLAVERY. It is a disgrace and blot on your free government and on a Christian State. We have nothing in Russia or Hungary which is so degrading,

One slaveholder, together with the cotton men of the north, fretted and vexed by their sudden and unenviable notoriety, foolishly attempted to obviate the impressions made by the book, by denouncing it as a lying fiction. Nay, one of the most affecting illustrations of pure and undefiled Christianity that ever proceeded from an uninspired pen, was gravely declared, by an organ of cotton divinity, to be an ANTI-CHRISTIAN book.* Truly, indeed, the wisdom of man is

and we have nothing which so crushes the mind. And more than this, we hear you have now a LAW, just passed by your National Assembly, which would disgrace the cruel code of the Czar. We hear of free men and women, hunted like dogs on your mountains, and sent back, without trial, to bondage worse than our serfs have ever known. We have, in Europe, many excuses in ancient evils and deep-laid prejudices, but you, the young and free people, in this age, to be passing again, afresh, such measures of unmitigated wrong!"—*Home life in Germany, by Charles Loving Brace.* Mr. Brace honestly adds: "*I must say that the blood tingled to my cheek with shame, as he spoke.*"

* "We have read the book, and regard it as Anti-Christian, on the same grounds that the chronicle regards it decidedly anti ministerial." —New York Observer, September 22, 1852.—*Editorial.* The Bishop of Rome also regards the book as Anti-Christian, and has forbidden his subjects to read it. On the other hand, the clergy of Great Britain differ most widely from the reverend gentlemen of the "Observer" and the Vatican, in their estimate of the character of the book. Said Dr. Wardlaw, who on this subject may be regarded as the representative of the Protestant Divines of Europe: "He who can read it without the breathings of devotion, must, if he call himself a Christian, have a Christianity as *unique and questionable* as his humanity."

foolishness with God. "He disappointeth the devices of the crafty."

Branded with falsehood and impiety, the author was happily put on her trial before the civilized world. She collected, arranged, and gave to the press, a mass of unimpeachable documents, consisting of laws, judicial decisions, trials, confessions of slaveholders, advertisements from southern papers, and testimonies of eye-witnesses. The proof was conclusive and overwhelming that the picture she had drawn of American slavery was unfaithful, only because the coloring was faint, and wanted the crimson dye of the original. A verdict of not guilty of exaggeration has been rendered by acclamation.

It has long been the standing refuge of the slaveholders, that northern men and Europeans, in condemning slavery, were passing judgment against an institution of which they were ignorant. The "peculiar institution" was represented as some great *mystery* which could not be understood beyond the slave region. Thanks to the fugitive law, it has led to the construction of a "*key*," which has unlocked our Republican bastile, thrown open to the sunlight its hideous dungeons, and exposed the various instruments of torture for subjecting the soul, as well as the body, to hopeless and unresisting bondage. The iniquity of our cherished institution is no longer a MYSTERY. All Christendom is now made familiar with it, and is sending forth a cry of indignant remonstrance and of taunting scorn. Such is the suppression of anti-slavery agitation given to the slaveholders by their northern friends—such the strength imparted by the fugitive slave law to the system of human bondage. How applicable to the inventors and supporters of that statute are the words of David, in regard to some politician of his own day: "Behold he travaileth with iniquity, and hath conceived mischief, and brought forth falsehood. He made a pit, and digged it, and is fallen into the ditch which he made. His mischief shall return upon his own head, and his violent dealing shall come down upon his own pate;" and then he adds, "I will praise the Lord." So also let the Christian bless and magnify HIM, who by his infinite wisdom brings good out of evil, and in the case of the fugitive law, HATH CAUSED THE WRATH OF MAN TO PRAISE HIM.

But there is still a *remainder* of wrath. The law is still on the Statute Book, and hungry politicians are promising that there it shall ever remain; and terrible threats come from the south, of the ruin that shall overwhelm the free States, should the law be repealed or rendered less abominable than at present. Yet, in spite of northern promises, and professions of security, and in spite of the great swelling words of the dealers in human flesh, the *practical*, like the moral working of the law, has been very far from what its authors anticipated. The law was passed the 18th September, 1850, and, in two years and nine months, not fifty slaves have been recovered under it—not an average of EIGHTEEN slaves a year! Poor compensation this to the slaveholders for making themselves a bye-word, a proverb, and a reproach to Christendom—for giving a new and mighty impulse to abolition, and for deepening the detestation felt by the true friends of liberty and humanity, for an institution asking and obtaining for its protection a law so repugnant to the moral sense of mankind. But while this artful and wicked law, with its army of ten-dollar judges, and marshals, and constables, and office-seekers, and politicians, with the President and his cabinet all striving to enforce it, "to the fullest extent," has restored to their masters not *eighteen slaves* a year; the escapes from the prison house have probably never been more numerous, nor the aid and sympathy afforded by Christians more abundant. Thus has THE REMAINDER OF WRATH BEEN RESTRAINED. In the marvellous conversion of this odious law into an anti-slavery agency, let us find a new motive for unceasing and unwearied agitation against slavery, and a new pledge of ultimate triumph.

William Jay

BEDFORD, June 1853.

Antoinette L. Brown.

The Size of Souls.

A QUAINT old writer describes a class of persons who have souls so very small that "500 of them could dance at once upon the point of a cambric needle." These wee people are often wrapped up in a lump of the very coarsest of human clay, ponderous enough to give them the semblance of full-grown men and women. A grain of mustard seed, buried in the heart of a mammoth pumpkin, would be no comparison to the little soul, sheathed in its full grown body. The contrast in size would be insufficient to convey an adequate impression; and the tiny soul has little of the mustard seed spiciness.

Yet if this mass of flesh is only wrapped up in a *white skin*, even though it is not nearly thick enough to conceal the grossness and coarseness of the veiled material, the poor "feeble folk" within will fancy that he really belongs to the natural variety of aristocratic humanity. He has the good taste to refuse condescension sufficient to allow him to eat at table with a Frederick Douglass, a Samuel R. Ward, or a Dr. Pennington. Poor light little soul! It can borrow a pair of flea's legs, and, hopping up to the magnificent lights of public opinion, sit looking down upon the whole colored race in sovereign contempt.

Take off the thin veneering of a white skin, substitute in its stead the real African ebony, and then place him side by side with one of the above-mentioned men. Measure intellect with intellect—eloquence with eloquence! Mental and moral infancy stand abashed in the presence of nature's noblemen!

So, mere complexion is elevated above character. Sensible men and women are not ashamed of the acknowledgment. The fact has a popular endorsement. People *sneer* at *you* if you are not ready to comprehend the fitness of the thing. If you cannot weigh mind in a balance with a moiety of coloring matter, and still let the mind be found wanting, expect, in America, to lose cast yourself for want of approved taste.

If sin is capable of being made to look mean,

narrow, contemptible—to exhibit itself in its character of thorough, unmitigated bitterness—it is when exhibited in the light of our "peculiar" prejudices. Mind, Godlike, immortal mind, with its burden of deathless thought, its comprehensive and discriminating reason, its brilliant wit, its genial humor, its store-house of thrilling memories—a voice of mingled power and pathos, words burning with the unconsuming fire of genius, virtues gathering in ripened beauty upon a brave heart, and moral integrity preeminent over all else—all this could not make a black man the social equal of a white coxcomb, even though his brain were as blank as white paper, and his heart as black as darkness concentrated. May heaven alleviate our undiluted stupidity!

ANTOINETTE L. BROWN.

Vincent Ogé

[Fragments of a poem hitherto unpublished, upon a revolt of the free persons of color, in the island of St. Domingo (now Hayti), in the years 1790–1.]

THERE is, at times, an evening sky—
  The twilight's gift—of sombre hue,
All checkered wild and gorgeously
  With streaks of crimson, gold and blue;—
A sky that strikes the soul with awe,
  And, though not brilliant as the sheen,
Which in the east at morn we saw,
  Is far more glorious, I ween;—
So glorious that, when night hath come
And shrouded it in deepest gloom,
We turn aside with inward pain
And pray to see that sky again.
Such sight is like the struggle made
When freedom bids unbare the blade,

And calls from every mountain-glen—
  From every hill—from every plain,
Her chosen ones to stand like men,
  And cleanse their souls from every stain
Which wretches, steeped in crime and blood,
Have cast upon the form of God.
Though peace like morning's golden hue,
  With blooming groves and waving fields,
Is mildly pleasing to the view,
  And all the blessings that it yields
Are fondly welcomed by the breast
  Which finds delight in passion's rest,
That breast with joy foregoes them all,
While listening to Freedom's call.
Though red the carnage,—though the strife
Be filled with groans of parting life,—
Though battle's dark, ensanguined skies
Give echo but to agonies—
  To shrieks of wild despairing,—
We willingly repress a sigh—
Nay, gaze with rapture in our eye,
Whilst "FREEDOM!" is the rally-cry
  That calls to deeds of daring.

* * * * * * * *

The waves dash brightly on thy shore,
  Fair island of the southern seas!
As bright in joy as when of yore
  They gladly hailed the Genoese,—
That daring soul who gave to Spain
A world—last trophy of her reign!
Basking in beauty, thou dost seem
A vision in a poet's dream!
Thou look'st as though thou claim'st not birth
With sea and sky and other earth,
That smile around thee but to show
Thy beauty in a brighter glow,—
That are unto thee as the foil
  Artistic hands have featly set
Around Golconda's radiant spoil,
  To grace some lofty coronet,—
A foil which serves to make the gem
The glory of that diadem!

* * * * * * * *

If Eden claimed a favored haunt,
  Most hallowed of that blessed ground,
Where tempting fiend with guileful taunt
  A resting-place would ne'er have found,—

As shadowing it well might seek
  The loveliest home in that fair isle,
Which in its radiance seemed to speak
  As to the charmed doth Beauty's smile,
That whispers of a thousand things
For which words find no picturings.
Like to the gifted Greek who strove
  To paint a crowning work of art,
And form his ideal Queen of Love,
  By choosing from each grace a part,
Blending them in one beauteous whole,
To charm the eye, transfix the soul,
And hold it in enraptured fires,
Such as a dream of heaven inspires,—
So seem the glad waves to have sought
  From every place its richest treasure,
And borne it to that lovely spot,
  To found thereon a home of pleasure;—
A home where balmy airs might float
  Through spicy bower and orange grove;
Where bright-winged birds might turn the note
  Which tells of pure and constant love;
Where earthquake stay its demon force,
And hurricane its wrathful course;

Where nymph and fairy find a home,
And foot of spoiler never come.
* * * * * * * *
And Ogé stands mid this array
  Of matchless beauty, but his brow
Is brightened not by pleasure's play;
  He stands unmoved—nay, saddened now,
As doth the lorn and mateless bird
That constant mourns, whilst all unheard,
The breezes freighted with the strains
Of other songsters sweep the plain,—
That ne'er breathes forth a joyous note,
Though odors on the zephyrs float—
The tribute of a thousand bowers,
Rich in their store of fragrant flowers.
Yet Ogé's was a mind that joyed
  With nature in her every mood,
Whether in sunshine unalloyed
  With darkness, or in tempest rude
And, by the dashing waterfall,
  Or by the gently flowing river,
Or listening to the thunder's call,
  He'd joy away his life forever.
But ah! life is a changeful thing,
  And pleasures swiftly pass away,

And we may turn, with shuddering,
  From what we sighed for yesterday.
The guest, at banquet-table spread
With choicest viands, shakes with dread,
Nor heeds the goblet bright and fair,
Nor tastes the dainties rich and rare,
Nor bids his eye with pleasure trace
The wreathed flowers that deck the place,
If he but knows there is a draught
Among the cordials, that, if quaffed,
Will send swift poison through his veins.
  So Ogé seems; nor does his eye
With pleasure view the flowery plains,
  The bounding sea, the spangled sky,
As, in the short and soft twilight,
  The stars peep brightly forth in heaven,
And hasten to the realms of night,
  As handmaids of the Even.

* * * * * * * *

The loud shouts from the distant town,
  Joined in with nature's gladsome lay;
The lights went glancing up and down,
  Riv'ling the stars—nay, seemed as they

Could stoop to claim, in their high home,
  A sympathy with things of earth,
And had from their bright mansions come,
  To join them in their festal mirth.
For the land of the Gaul had arose in its might,
And swept by as the wind of a wild, wintry night;
And the dreamings of greatness—the phantoms of
  power,
Had passed in its breath like the things of an hour.
Like the violet vapors that brilliantly play
Round the glass of the chemist, then vanish away,
The visions of grandeur which dazzlingly shone,
Had gleamed for a time, and all suddenly gone.
And the fabric of ages—the glory of kings,
Accounted most sacred mid sanctified things,
Reared up by the hero, preserved by the sage,
And drawn out in rich hues on the chronicler's page,
Had sunk in the blast, and in ruins lay spread,
While the altar of freedom was reared in its stead.
And a spark from that shrine in the free-roving
  breeze,
Had crossed from fair France to that isle of the s[illegible]
And a flame was there kindled which fitfully shone
Mid the shout of the free, and the dark captive's groan;

As, mid contrary breezes, a torch-light will play,
Now streaming up brightly—now dying away.

* * * * * * * *

The reptile slumbers in the stone,
  Nor dream we of his pent abode;
The heart conceals the anguished groan,
  With all the poignant griefs that goad
            The brain to madness;
Within the hushed volcano's breast,
  The molten fires of ruin lie;—
Thus human passions seem at rest,
  And on the brow serene and high,
            Appears no sadness.
But still the fires are raging there,
Of vengeance, hatred, and despair;
And when they burst, they wildly pour
  Their lava flood of woe and fear,
And in one short—one little hour,
  Avenge the wrongs of many a year.

* * * * * * * *

And Ogé standeth in his hall;
  But now he standeth not alone;—
A brother 's there, and friends; and all
  Are kindred spirits with his own;

For mind will join with kindred mind,
As matter's with its like combined.
They speak of wrongs they had received—
Of freemen, of their rights bereaved;
And as they pondered o'er the thought
Which in their minds so madly wrought,
Their eyes gleamed as the lightning's flash,
Their words seemed as the torrent's dash
That falleth, with a low, deep sound,
Into some dark abyss profound,—
A sullen sound that threatens more
Than other torrents' louder roar.
Ah! they had borne well as they might,
  Such wrongs as freemen ill can bear;
And they had urged both day and night,
  In fitting words, a freeman's prayer;
And when the heart is filled with grief,
  For wrongs of all true souls accurst,
In action it must seek relief,
  Or else, o'ercharged, it can but burst.
Why blame we them, if they oft spake
Words that were fitted to awake
The soul's high hopes—its noblest parts—
The slumbering passions of brave hearts,

And send them as the simoom's breath,
Upon a work of woe and death?
And woman's voice is heard amid
  The accents of that warrior train;
And when has woman's voice e'er bid,
  And man could from its hest refrain?
Hers is the power o'er his soul
  That 's never wielded by another,
And she doth claim this soft control
  As sister, mistress, wife, or mother.
So sweetly doth her soft voice float
  O'er hearts by guilt or anguish riven,
It seemeth as a magic note
  Struck from earth's harps by hands of heaven.
And there 's the mother of Ogé,
  Who with firm voice, and steady heart,
And look unaltered, well can play
  The Spartan mother's hardy part;
And send her sons to battle-fields,
  And bid them come in triumph home,
Or stretched upon their bloody shields,
  Rather than bear the bondman's doom.
" Go forth," she said, " to victory;
Or else, go bravely forth to die!

Go forth to fields where glory floats
In every trumpet's cheering notes!
Go forth, to where a freeman's death
Glares in each cannon's fiery breath!
Go forth and triumph o'er the foe;
Or failing that, with pleasure go
To molder on the battle-plain,
Freed ever from the tyrant's chain!
But if your hearts should craven prove,
Forgetful of your zeal—your love
For rights and franchises of men,
My heart will break; but even then,
Whilst bidding life and earth adieu,
This be the prayer I'll breathe for you:
'Passing from guilt to misery,
May this for aye your portion be,—
A life, dragged out beneath the rod—
An end, abhorred of man and God—
As monument, the chains you nurse—
As epitaph, your mother's curse!'"

* * * * * *

A thousand hearts are breathing high,
And voices shouting "Victory!"
Which soon will hush in death;

The trumpet clang of joy that speaks,
Will soon be drowned in the shrieks
Of the wounded's stifling breath,
The tyrant's plume in dust lies low—
Th' oppressed has triumphed o'er his foe.
But ah! the lull in the furious blast
May whisper not of ruin past;
It may tell of the tempest hurrying on,
To complete the work the blast begun.
he voice of a Syren, it may whisp'ringly tell
oment of hope in the deluge of rain;
the shout of the free heart may rapt'rously swell,
While the tyrant is gath'ring his power again.
Though the balm of the leech may soften the smart,
It never can turn the swift barb from its aim;
And thus the resolve of the true freeman's heart
May not keep back his fall, though it free it from shame.
Though the hearts of those heroes all well could accord
With freedom's most noble and loftiest word;
Their virtuous strength availeth them nought
With the power and skill that the tyrant brought.
Gray veterans trained in many a field
Where the fate of nations with blood was sealed,

In Italia's vales—on the shores of the Rhine—
Where the plains of fair France give birth to the vine—
Where the Tagus, the Ebro, go dancing along,
Made glad in their course by the Muleteer's song—
All these were poured down in the pride of their
might,
On the land of Ogé, in that terrible fight.
Ah! dire was the conflict, and many the slain,
Who slept the last sleep on that red battle-plain!
The flash of the cannon o'er valley and height
Danced like the swift fires of a northern night,
Or the quivering glare which leaps forth as a token
That the King of the Storm from his cloud-throne
has spoken.
And oh! to those heroes how welcome the fate
Of Sparta's brave sons in Thermopylæ's strait;
With what ardor of soul they then would have given
Their last look at earth for a long glance at heaven!
Their lives to their country—their backs to the sod—
Their heart's blood to the sword, and their souls to
their God!
But alas! although many lie silent and slain,
More blest are they far than those clanking the
chain,

In the hold of the tyrant, debarrèd from the day;—
And among these sad captives is Vincent Ogé!

* * * * * * * *

Another day's bright sun has risen,
And shines upon the insurgent's prison;
Another night has slowly passed,
And Ogé smiles, for 'tis the last
He'll droop beneath the tyrant's power—
The galling chains! Another hour,
And answering to the jailor's call,
He stands within the Judgment Hall.
They've gathered there;—they who have pressed
Their fangs into the soul distressed,
To pain its passage to the tomb
With mock'ry of a legal doom.
They've gathered there;—they who have stood
Firmly and fast in hour of blood,—
Who've seen the lights of hope all die,
As stars fade from a morning sky,—
They've gathered there, in that dark hour—
The latest of the tyrant's power,—
An hour that speaketh of the day
Which never more shall pass away,—

The glorious day beyond the grave,
Which knows no master—owns no slave.
And there, too, are the rack—the wheel—
The torturing screw—the piercing steel,—
Grim powers of death all crusted o'er
With other victims' clotted gore.
Frowning they stand, and in their cold,
Silent solemnity, unfold
The strong one's triumph o'er the weak—
The awful groan—the anguished shriek—
The unconscious mutt'rings of despair—
The strained eyeball's idiot stare—
The hopeless clench—the quiv'ring frame—
The martyr's death—the despot's shame.
The rack—the tyrant—victim,—all
Are gathered in that Judgment Hall.
Draw we the veil, for 'tis a sight
But friends can gaze on with delight.
The sunbeams on the rack that play,
For sudden terror flit away
From this dread work of war and death,
As angels do with quickened breath,
From some dark deed of deepest sin,
Ere they have drunk its spirit in.

* * * * * * * *

No mighty host with banners flying,
  Seems fiercer to a conquered foe,
Than did those gallant heroes dying,
  To those who gloated o'er their woe ;—
Grim tigers, who have seized their prey,
Then turn and shrink abashed away;
And, coming back and crouching nigh,
Quail 'neath the flashing of the eye,
Which tells that though the life has started,
The will to strike has not departed.

* * * * * * * *

Sad was your fate, heroic band!
Yet mourn we not, for yours' the stand
Which will secure to you a fame,
That never dieth, and a name
That will, in coming ages, be
A signal word for Liberty.
Upon the slave's o'erclouded sky,
  Your gallant actions traced the bow,
Which whispered of deliv'rance nigh—
  The meed of one decisive blow.
Thy coming fame, Ogé! is sure;
Thy name with that of L'Ouverture,

And all the noble souls that stood
With both of you, in times of blood,
Will live to be the tyrant's fear—
Will live, the sinking soul to cheer!

George B. Vashon.

SYRACUSE, N. Y., August 31st, 1853.

The Law of Liberty.

FREEDOM, under the proper restraint of Law and Duty, is a *political* good, for that which is morally wrong can never be politically right.

Fine moral sense will pour indignation on oppression, as well as applause on worth. It will give sympathy to the afflicted, and treasures to relieve the needy. Such a spirit will exalt a nation, and command the respect of other nations. But general freedom can only flourish beneath the undisturbed dominion of equitable laws.

Governments should aim at the welfare of the people, and that government which secures the person, the property, the liberty, the lives of dutiful subjects, and thus makes the common good the rule and measure of its government, will receive a blessing from God.

Let America act on her own avowed principles, that every man is born free, and she will be exalted, when tyrannical, persecuting, slaveholding nations will come to nought.

Wm Marsh DD

H. CANON OF WORCESTER.

The Swiftness of Time in God.

FROM THE KNABEN WUNDERHORN. (B. I. p. 73, *et seq.*)

THE general at Grosswardein
Had once a little daughter fine:—
Her name was called Theresia,—
God-loving, modest, chaste and fair:

And from her childhood up was she
Most deeply given to piety,
With prayers and music's solemn tone
She ever praised the Three-in-One.

Whene'er she heard of Jesus' name,
Her love and joy flamed brighter flame;
Jesus to serve she makes her cross,
Devotes herself to be his Spouse.

A noble lord came her to woo,
Her father gave consent thereto;

The mother to her daughter said,—
"Dear child, this man thou'lt surely wed."

The daughter said, "Mother of me
That can and must not ever be.
My heart is fixed on higher worth,
A Bridegroom he not of this earth."

The mother then, "My daughter dear,
Ah, do not contradict us here,
Thy sire and I we both are old,
And God has blessed our toil with gold."

Thereat the maid began to weep,
"I have a lover beloved so deep,
To him I've made my promise down;
I'll wear for him a virgin crown."

Thereat the sire, "This must not be,
My child away this phantasy,
Where wilt thou dwell when past thy prime?
We both are old, far gone in time!"

The noble lord again draws near,
And even the bridal feast prepare,

For all things soon were ready made,—
But sorrow veils the maiden's head.

Quick to the garden, goeth she,
There falls she down upon her knee,
Out from her heart her prayer she poured
To Jesus her espoused Lord.

She lay before him on her face,
And sighed with sighs to win his grace.
The dearest Christ the clouds unrolled,
"Look up," said he, "my maid behold!

"Thou yet shalt be, in briefest time,
In heaven with me in joy's full prime,
And mid the lovely angels there,
In full delight and joy appear."

He greets the maiden wondrous fair:
She stands before him without fear,
Down cast her eyes with modest grace,—
She felt the beauty of his face.

Then speaks the youth, the heavenly King,
And weds her with a golden ring;—

"Look there, my bride! Love's pledge for thee,
Oh, wear it on thy hand for me."

The maiden then sweet vows took,
"My Bridegroom dear!" to Christ she spoke,
"Herewith art thou firm wed to me,
Henceforth my heart loves none but thee."

Then walked abroad the married pair,
And gathered many a blossom fair;—
Jesus thus spake to her anew:—
"Come, and my lovely garden view!"

He took the maiden by the hand,
And led her from her fatherland,
Unto his Father's garden fair
Where many beauteous blossoms are.

The maiden now with joy may win
The precious fruits which grow therein;
But mortal fancy cannot know
The noble fruits therein which grow.

She hears such music and such song,
That length of time seems nothing long,

And silver-white the brooklets there
Flow ever on so pure and fair.

The youth again addressed the maid,
"My garden here thou hast surveyed.
I will again conduct thee home.
To thine own land, the time is come."

The maiden turns with grief away,
Comes to the town without delay,
The watchman calls, "Stand, who goes there?"
She says, "I to my father must repair!"

"Who is your father, then," quoth he,
"The general," she answers free.
The watchman then replied and smiled,
"The general;—he has no child."

But by her garments all men see,
The maiden is of high degree.
The watchman then conducts her straight
Before the guardians of the State.

The maid declares and stands thereto,
The general is her father true.

And but two hours have scarcely flown,
Since she went out to walk alone.

The guardians saw a wonder great,
And asked where she had been of late;
Her father's name, his power and race,
That she must tell them face to face.

They searched the ancient records through,
And this they found was written true,
That once was lost a bride so fine
From this same city Grosswardein.

The length of time they came to try,
And sixteen years they find passed by;
And yet the maid was fresh and fair,
As when first in her fifteenth year.

Thereby the guardians understand
This is the work of God's own hand.
They bring the maiden food to eat,
She turns white as a winding-sheet.

"Of earthly things I wish for nought,"
Cries she; "but let a priest be brought,

That I may take ere death is sent,
The body true in sacrament.

As soon as this last act was done—
And many a Christian looked thereon—
Free from all pain and mortal smart,
Then ceased to beat that holy heart.

Theo. Parker

Visit of a Fugitive Slave to the Grave of Wilberforce.

ON a beautiful morning in the month of June, while strolling about Trafalgar Square, I was attracted to the base of the Nelson column, where a crowd was standing gazing at the bas-relief representations of some of the great naval exploits of the man whose statue stands on the top of the pillar. The death-wound which the hero received on board the Victory, and his being carried from the ship's deck by his companions, is executed with great skill. Being no admirer of warlike heroes, I was on the point of turning away, when I perceived among the figures (which were as large as life) a full-blooded African, with as white a set of teeth as ever I had seen, and all the other peculiarities of feature that distinguish that race from the rest of the human family, with

Wm W. Brown.

musket in hand and a dejected countenance, which told that he had been in the heat of the battle, and shared with the other soldiers the pain in the loss of their commander. However, as soon as I saw my sable brother, I felt more at home, and remained longer than I had intended. Here was the Negro, as black a man as was ever imported from the coast of Africa, represented in his proper place by the side of Lord Nelson, on one of England's proudest monuments. How different, thought I, was the position assigned to the colored man on similar monuments in the United States. Some years since, while standing under the shade of the monument erected to the memory of the brave Americans who fell at the storming of Fort Griswold, Connecticut, I felt a degree of pride as I beheld the names of two Africans who had fallen in the fight, yet I was grieved but not surprised to find their names colonized off, and a line drawn between them and the whites. This was in keeping with American historical injustice to its colored heroes.

The conspicuous place assigned to this representative of an injured race, by the side of one of England's greatest heroes, brought vividly before my eye the wrongs of Africa and the philanthropic man of Great Britain, who had labored so long and so successfully for the abolition of the slave trade, and the emancipation of the slaves of the West Indies; and I at once resolved to pay a visit to the grave of Wilberforce.

A half an hour after, I entered Westminster Abbey, at Poets' Corner, and proceeded in search of the patriot's tomb; I had, however, gone but a few steps, when I found myself in front of the tablet erected to the memory of Granville Sharpe, by the African Institution of London, in 1816; upon the marble was a long inscription, recapitulating many of the deeds of this benevolent man, and from which I copied the following:—"He aimed to rescue his native country from the guilt and inconsistency of employing the arm of freedom to rivet the fetters of bondage, and establish for the negro race, in the person of Somerset, the long-disputed rights of human nature. Having in this glorious cause triumphed over the combined resistance of interest, prejudice, and pride, he took his post among the foremost of the honorable band associated to deliver Africa from the rapacity of Europe, by the abolition of the slave-trade; nor was death permitted to interrupt his career of usefulness, till he had witnessed that act of the British Parliament by which the abolition was decreed." After viewing minutely the profile of this able defender of the negro's rights, which was finely chiselled on the tablet, I took a hasty glance at Shakspeare, on the one side, and Dryden on the other, and then passed on, and was soon in the north aisle, looking upon the mementoes placed in honor of genius. There stood a grand and expressive monument to Sir Isaac Newton, which was in every way worthy of the great man to whose memory it was erected. A short distance from that was a statue to Addison, representing the great writer clad in his morning gown, looking as if he had just left the study, after finishing some chosen article for the *Spectator*. The stately monument to the Earl of Chatham is the most attractive in this part of the Abbey. Fox, Pitt, Grattan, and many others, are here represented by monuments. I had to stop at the splendid marble erected to the memory of Sir Fowell Buxton, Bart. A long inscription enumerates his many good qualities, and concludes by saying:—" This monument is erected by his friends and fellow-laborers, at home and abroad, assisted by the grateful contributions of many thousands of the African race." A few steps further and I was standing over the ashes of Wilberforce. In no other place so small do so many great men lie together. The following is the inscription on the monument erected to the memory of this devoted friend of the oppressed and degraded negro race:—

"To the memory of WILLIAM WILBERFORCE, born in Hull, August 24, 1759, died in London, July 29, 1833. For nearly half a century a member of the House of Commons, and for six parliaments during that period, one of the two representatives for Yorkshire. In an age and country fertile in great and good men, he was among the foremost of those who fixed the character of their times; because to high and various talents, to warm benevolence, and to universal candor, he added the abiding eloquence of a Christian life. Eminent as he was in every department of public labor, and a leader in every work of charity, whether to relieve the temporal or the spiritual wants of his fellow men, his name will ever be specially identified with those exertions which, by the blessings of God, removed from England the guilt of the African slave-trade, and prepared the way for the abolition of slavery in every colony of the empire. In the prosecution of these objects, he relied not in vain on God; but, in the progress, he was called to endure great obloquy and great opposition. He outlived, however, all enmity, and, in the evening of his days, withdrew from public life and public observation, to the bosom of his family. Yet he died not unnoticed or forgotten by his country; the Peers and Commons of England, with the Lord Chancellor and the Speaker at their head, in solemn procession from their respective houses, carried him to his fitting place among the mighty dead around, here to repose, till, through the merits of Jesus Christ his only Redeemer and Saviour, whom in his life and in his writings he had desired to glorify, he shall rise in the resurrection of the just."

The monument is a fine one; his figure is seated on a pedestal, very ingeniously done, and truly expressive of his age, and the pleasure he seemed to derive from his own thoughts. Either the orator or the poet have said or sung the praises of most of the great men who lie buried in Westminster Abbey, in enchanting strains. The statues of heroes, princes, and statesmen are there to proclaim their power, worth, or brilliant genius, to posterity. But as time shall step between them and the future, none will be sought after with more enthusiasm or greater pleasure than that of Wilberforce. No man's philosophy was ever moulded in a nobler cast than his; it was founded in the school of Christianity, which was, that all men are by nature equal; that they are wisely and justly endowed by their Creator with certain rights which are irrefragable, and no matter how human pride and avarice may depress and debase, still God is the author of good to man; and of evil, man is the artificer to himself and to his species. Unlike Plato and Socrates, his mind was free from the gloom that surrounded theirs. Let the name, the worth, the zeal, and other excellent qualifications of this noble man, ever live in our hearts, let his deeds ever be the theme of our praise, and let us teach our children to honor and love the name of Willliam Wilberforce.

W. Wells Brown.

LONDON.

Narrative of Albert and Mary.

IT was a beautiful morning as ever glittered over the broad Atlantic. The sun had the brightness and the sky the soft cerulean with which the month of June adorns the latitude of Carolina. The sea was not heavy nor rolling, but its motion was just enough to make its waves sparkle under the slanting rays of the morning sun.

Mary stood with her betrothed in the bow of the boat, as it gracefully ploughed its way towards New York. She was only eighteen, and Albert was just twenty.

Mary was on her way to Troy, to complete her studies in the excellent institution for young ladies, which has sent out some of the brightest ornaments of their sex, to refine and bless the world. She had been entrusted to Albert's care, who was to spend his summer in New York, in the pursuit of the legal profession. They were both Carolinians, and had no little of that ardent spirit which distinguishes the youth of the South; while their well-developed forms, their intellectual countenances, and their sensible speech, placed them in association beyond their years.

As Mary leaned upon the arm of her gallant protector, their conversation sparkled as the ocean spray that dashed against steamer's bow. But suddenly, as the jet black eye of Albert Gillon caught the soft blue of Mary's, he started at the discovery of a tear trembling upon her eye-lash.

"Sweet Mary, what saddens you?"

"Ah! Albert, the greatest trial of my feelings is the thought that you have never yet consecrated yourself to Christ."

"I have," replied Albert, "no natural repugnance to religion. On the contrary, I see and acknowledge God in all his works and in all his providence, as the author and supreme ruler of all things. But, Mary, I do not understand the God of the Bible. I do not understand how they who claim to be God's own people, and have the distinguishing title of Christians, are, many of them, far worse in moral character, than those who make no such profession. I do not mean hypocrites; but those who are actually respected as orthodox Christians. There is Mr. Verse, of Philadelphia, for instance, who has a high place as a religious editor, and discusses the doctrines of Christianity with a zeal which shows he takes deep interest in his work, and yet young as I am, and gay as I am, I can see that in his practical application of Christianity, he teaches sentiments at variance with the plainest principles of moral truth; and he sets himself against those whose moral character is above reproach; and rebukes them as infidels in their very efforts to elevate the moral tone of society. How is it that Mr. Verse is recognized as a Christian, and these excellent men are avoided as infidels? Why is he fit for heaven, and they must be cast down to hell? I don't understand it."

"I know," replied Mary, "that wiser heads than mine find difficulty in answering your question; and it would be presumptuous in me to signify that I can solve it to your satisfaction. But still, Albert, your observations only confirm, in my own mind, your total ignorance of what constitutes a Christian. Albert, it is not morality; it is not consistency of practice with profession; it is not the *doing* right that makes a Christian, for if man could have attained to entire correctness in morals, there would have been no such thing as Christianity. But it is because of man's wickedness and his inconsistency, both in theory and in practice, that the Christian religion is presented as the means of attaining to *salvation.* Christ makes the Christian—the Christian in Christ and Christ in the Christian—a loving, affectionate, endearing union—of ignorance with wisdom, of infirmity with strength, of immorality with virtue. Christ throws his robe of righteousness over the follies and the wickedness of the converted soul, and by covering him with himself, gradually similates him to himself until what is carnal being cast off, the spiritual remains at death a pure child of God."

"Dear me, Mary, you look lovely as you speak this mysterious theology. And I really pant after such feelings as I see beaming from your countenance; but you might just as well speak to me in Arabic for any understanding I can have of this thing called Christianity. It must be something good, or it could not thus fill your own soul, intelligent as you are, with a joy that makes you indifferent to those gaieties of life which give me pleasure."

"You need," said Mary, "the teachings of God's spirit. You know I took delight in those things a year ago, but God's spirit taught me that I was sinning in partaking of them. I was at Fayolle's, dancing, and, in the midst of a figure in the cotillon, my head became giddy, and I had to be supported to a seat. I soon recovered, but the thought of a sudden death distressed me, for it came very forcibly to my mind—I am a wicked sinner."

"O, Mary, Mary," interrupted Albert, "you did not think yourself a sinner!"

"Yes, Albert, I did. I had never thought so before, but had rather prided myself upon being called a good girl by all my acquaintances. But I now saw things in a different light; and when I went home and began self-examination, I soon found I had a very wicked heart. I tried to do better, but the more I tried to live unto God the more I discovered the proneness of my heart to sin. I tried to think good thoughts, and evil thoughts came directly in my way to mar my peace. Day after day I made effort to purify my thoughts. It was all in vain. A pure thought immediately suggested its opposite, and I found myself more familiar with the evil than the good. It shocked me. But I penetrated deeper and deeper into my own heart—into the iniquity of my soul, until I despaired of ever sounding its depth. I then cried to God to have mercy on me. He heard my prayer, and Jesus Christ came to my help. I felt that he had suffered in my stead, and had poured out his blood as an atonement for my sins. I found peace to my soul as I cast myself, a poor, helpless sinner, upon his atoning altar, and bathed myself in his all-cleansing blood."

Mary could proceed no farther, for the tears began to flow too rapidly, and her emotion might have been noticed by others than Albert.

The wind, too, began to rise, and it blew so fresh that they retired to the cabin, where Albert occupied himself with a game of chess, and Mary read, with evident pleasure, such parts of her dearly-prized Bible which suited the state of her mind, occasionally calling Albert's attention to some passage particularly striking.

In the afternoon, Mary took her seat in a position to enjoy the best view of the western sky, in which floated, in all their gorgeousness, the variegated sun-lit clouds.

Albert soon joined her. "Well, Mary, you seem to be meditating; but allow me to participate in the luxury of your reflections upon that splendid horizon."

"Indeed, Albert, I was thinking how much more impressive is such scenery than the traveller on land enjoys. In the rapid succession of scenery and variety of faces, as the coach or the steam car drives rapidly onward, everything one sees increases the mind's confusion. Whatever he casts his eye upon, worthy of admiration, attracts his attention but a moment; and the sublimity of mountain heights, the gaudy decorations of fertile valleys, and the frowning grandeur of rocks, as they cast their dark shadow upon some foaming torrent, flit by him as a dream of twilight, and leave upon his memory only pencil outlines of the beautiful and the sublime. Not so the voyager on the ocean. Here the beautiful imprints itself ineffaceably in all its sparkling and its gorgeous variety upon the enchanted mind, and the grand and the sublime raise such a tempest of wonder in the soul that the ocean ever after rolls its foaming waves over the broad expanse of memory."

"Mary," said Albert, "these clouds, floating so gracefully on the ocean, and this gorgeous horizon inspiring your poetic fancy, are something more than mere sky drapery, for you'll perceive that the wind is becoming boisterous, and I fear we are going to have a stormy night."

"You do not feel alarmed, do you Albert?"

"I cannot say I feel alarmed; but I would be more comfortable at this time if I had not so precious a charge. There may be no real danger, but there can be no harm in preparing for what might happen. If we should have a storm I wish you would take your seat on that large box, so as to appropriate it and keep it. Your father brought me two life-preservers and a good cord, when we came on board, and charged me to use them in case of accident. You smile, Mary, at my earnestness, and perhaps my love for you induces anxiety which circumstances do not warant. Still you can keep in mind my directions."

Albert walked towards the bow of the steamer, while Mary again fixed her attention upon the variegated clouds. She did not participate in Albert's apprehensions, and thought his anxiety needless. Yet his earnest request made that sort of impression upon her mind which rather conduced to religious contemplation.

The broad disk of the sun could be seen through the floating cloud, and as Albert returned, Mary remarked:—"Albert, an hour ago I tried to look at the sun, but his light dazzled my eyes to blindness. I could not mark its shape nor perceive its beauty. But now the cloud floats before it, and through its light vapor I see the sun's circular infinity, and admire its beauty and its glory undazzled by its effulgence. So it is I see God through Christ, as he transmits the glory of his Father. And it is by thus seeing God through Christ, instead of by the eyes of intellect and mere mental observation, that I obtain hope in God and feel prepared to enter upon the realities of that world which is eternally lighted by the invisible presence of Jehovah. Seeing him in Christ Jesus, I feel an assurance of his mercy, and am freed from those apprehensions which your scepticism and distrust occasion yourself."

"My dear Mary," replied Albert, "do not suppose my counsel to you originated in any fear for myself personally. It may be from want of reflection, but really I do not know what the fear of death is. Your safety, Mary, is the cause of my present anxiety. I do not doubt your preparation for eternity, but I am not willing to resign you yet to the companionship of angels. If you perish beneath these billows, and I survive, my hope for happiness in this life is blasted. What is to be beyond the grave I know not; and my religion concerns the life that now is. I must make the best of time, and leave eternity to be taken account of when I am fairly launched into it. Perhaps enjoying this world with you, I might learn from you to prepare for eternity. At present my care must be to get my dear Mary safely over this treacherous ocean."

The sun now sank beneath the western horizon. The variegated colors of the sky were rapidly commingling into one dense canopy of gloom.

The passengers earnestly inquired of the captain about the prospect. He hoped to run into the port of Wilmington, but he exhorted them to have brave hearts for the danger was imminent. The storm was rapidly increasing. All urged that the pressure of steam be increased to the utmost capacity of the boat.

O, what an anxious crowd were upon the deck of that steamer, as they strained their eyes towards the land, and anon lost their balance by the dashing of ''lows! The lightning played with terrific splen- rnating with the blackness of the heavens; the roar of the waves was only hushed by the wful artillery of the skies.

Mary was sitting where Albert had directed, awaiting with great calmness the result of the storm.

Albert carefully fastened her with a cord to the box, having first placed beneath her arms the life-preserver. Placing another life-preserver around himself, he stood by Mary's side with watchful anxiety. Suddenly a heavy sea threw the boat forcibly to one side, and Albert mechanically stretching forth his hand to save himself, accidentally got caught in the rope that he had entwined about the box, and with Mary was tossed into the sea and overwhelmed with the waves.

The steamer was several hundred yards ahead of them before Albert succeeded in adjusting his position to maintain a good hold upon the box. His first thought was to examine how Mary was situated. The lightning gave him sufficient assurance that she was alive and unhurt. At that moment a dreadful explosion directed their eyes towards the steamer, and the awful sight was exhibited of their late associates blown into the air and then sinking beneath the waves.

The loss of the Pulaski has made many a flowing tear. But few were left to tell the horrors of that night. The public are familiar with their description of the sad disaster. But they knew not the fate of Albert and Mary, and only added them to the catalogue of the lost

It was with the greatest difficulty that Albert could afford his charge any aid, and they must both soon have perished if the storm had been long protracted. But fortunately, the wind shifting, the clouds were soon dispersed, and the stars shone out brightly.

Before morning they were rescued from their perilous situation, and found themselves, on recovering from their exhaustion, in the comfortable cabin of a fast-sailing brig. The storm, although exceedingly perilous to a steamboat, was not such as to damage a well-trimmed vessel; and the brig, soon after the explosion, bore down towards the wreck, and recovered from a watery grave the interesting subjects of our narrative.

Mary was taken on board in a state of entire unconsciousness, while Albert was too much interested for her to make any special observation of the persons by whom they were rescued.

After seeing her sufficiently restored to animation to be left to repose, he retired from her state-room and suffered himself to be assisted to a berth.

The sun was high in the heavens when they were awaked from their slumber and invited to breakfast. Every accommodation in the way of dry clothing was supplied them, and they met in the saloon of the brig to embrace, in the transport of grateful hearts.

Having recovered their self-possession, they looked around for their deliverers. None were in the saloon with them but a highly-accomplished looking lady and the steward and stewardess.

The lady saluted them in the blandest and most refined manner, and expressed her sincere gratification that they had been so soon delivered from their perilous situation, and were already so well recovered from their exhaustion.

"To whom, Madam," said Albert, "are we indebted for these expressions of kindness and tender solicitude?"

"I am, sir, the wife of the captain and master of this brig. My husband will pay you his respects as soon as you have partaken of some of this warm Java and these hot rolls."

"I would not," said Mary, "be doing justice to my own feelings were I to sit down to breakfast without first asking your liberty, Madam, to read a beautiful psalm which occurs to my mind at this moment."

"Certainly," said the lady; "and, steward, invite the chaplain in to offer prayer. Doubtless it will be perfectly agreeable to our young guests."

A reverend and benevolent looking gentleman, in black, soon entered from the deck, and, in the kindest manner and address, saluted the young couple, expressing, with deep emotion, his sympathy with them and his anxiety in their behalf.

Mary pointed out to him the Psalm she had selected. He read it; made a few highly-appropriate comments, and, while all knelt, such a strain of grateful praise and of fervent prayer flowed from the lips of the warm-hearted minister as seldom is surpassed.

Mr. Gracelius, for this was the minister's name, was of the orthodox faith, and had long been engaged in preaching the doctrines of the Calvinistic school. Yet he was not bigoted or rigid. His heart was full of the milk of human kindness, and he carried conviction to his hearers, not more by the strength of his logic than the benignity of his address. He was just such a minister as the devout and accomplished Mary St. Clair would have full confidence in. She was delighted to think that she had been so fortunate as to meet such a friend and spiritual counsellor at such a time; and she at once gave utterance to the warm feelings of her heart, and begged that Mr. Gracelius would feel at perfect liberty to counsel and advise her.

"My advice then is, my dear young sister, that first of all you sit down to your breakfast, and allow Mrs. Templeton to help you and the young gentleman to your coffee."

Albert and Mary could not but feel that they had fallen among true friends. And, having eaten a cheerful breakfast, they both expressed their sincere gratitude to their kind hostess, which she received with equally deep emotion.

Captain Templeton now entered, and with great courteousness, blended with warmth of address, gave his hand to Albert, and, with a graceful bow to Mary, expressed the pleasure he felt in having rescued them from a watery grave. "And now, my young friends," said the Captain, "I wish you to make yourselves perfectly at home in my vessel; and as soon as I can with safety restore you to your friends, I shall do so."

"Permit me to inquire," said Albert, "to what port you are destined?"

"We do not go into any harbor in the United States," replied the Captain; "but should we meet with a merchant vessel under favorable circumstances, you will be placed on board."

"Is not this a merchant vessel?" inquired Albert.

"No, sir. This is an armed brig."

"Of what nation?" asked Albert.

The Captain smiled as, with a courteous bow, he replied, "We are pirates;" and immediately went on deck, leaving Albert and Mary in perfect amazement.

Recovering himself in a moment, Albert said to Mrs. Templeton: "Your husband is very jocose!"

"No, sir; he was serious in what he said. We are pirates. But you need be under no apprehension of danger, nor feel the slightest alarm. I know that you have been trained to believe that pirates are necessarily devoid of humane feelings, and are ever thirsting for blood. But I trust we are as hospitable and kind a people to our guests, as are to be found on land."

Albert and Mary were indeed the guests of a piratical crew; but they were soon relieved of all apprehension of personal danger; for there was that in the deportment of all on board which satisfied them of a sincere desire to serve and accommodate them in every way.

A few days brought them into such intimacy with the crew that they spoke with freedom, even on the subject of piracy. They were indeed astonished to find that even Mr. Gracelius advocated the claims of pirates as a civilized and religious people.

On board the brig they had morning and evening prayers, and a lecture one evening in the week, and two sermons on the Sabbath. What seemed particularly remarkable was the sound evangelical faith of the Captain and his family, and the unexceptionable doctrines that were preached by their minister. There was so much fervor, earnestness, and pathos in the sermons of Mr. Gracelius, that Mary was constrained to admit to Mrs. Templeton that she had never heard better.

They had been on the brig about three weeks,

without any event calculated to disturb the sensibilities of our young friends, beyond the unaccountably strange sentiments of the piratical crew. Everything was conducted with so much order and propriety, good taste and moral deportment, that they could scarcely believe at times otherwise than that a mere sportive hoax was being played upon them.

But the tranquil, social pastimes were now interrupted by a new scene of action.

It was a pleasant morning; a gentle breeze filled the sails. An unusual arrangement of the vessel attracted the attention of Albert. Soon he observed men at the guns, and Captain Templeton standing in a commanding position. The brig was bearing down upon a French merchantman.

Albert hastened to Mary, and disclosed to her the state of things. Mary at first trembled, but soon composed herself with trust in God. Albert, taking her arm into his, led her to where Captain Templeton was standing:

"Captain," said Albert, "I perceive you are bearing down upon that merchant vessel. Is it your object to place us on board, or do you design to capture her?"

"Mr. Gillon," replied the Captain, "I shall see to it that you and your young charge are safely provided for; and that you may be perfectly easy on that score, I now inform you that when I take possession of that merchantman, I shall make arrangements for you to be taken in her to a suitable port, whence you can find your way to your friends. Be composed now, and pay such attention to Miss St. Clair as the unusual occasion may seem in your judgment to require. In a few moments we shall have something to do, and perhaps a necessity to use our guns. But I hope not. If you will retire to the cabin, Mrs. Templeton will entertain you there better than you are likely to be on deck."

There was so much politeness in the Captain's manner, and yet evident fixedness of purpose, that Albert attempted no answer. There was now no doubt that their hospitable entertainers were pirates. They retired to the cabin, and sat there in profound silence. Soon Mrs. Templeton came in, and in her gentle winning manner began to prepare Mary for the scenes that might transpire.

"You must not be alarmed, my dear. You will be perfectly safe. I only regret we are so soon likely to lose your company."

"O Mrs. Templeton!" said Mary, "how can you prosecute such a life! It is so wicked! Excuse me, ma'am, but I cannot suppress my feelings of horror."

At this moment the conversation was interrupted by the entrance of Captain Templeton, who, with a calm countenance, said:—

"Wife, I perceive that there are several guns on that vessel, and I judge that the crew and passengers are somewhat numerous. We shall have to proceed with caution, and as we are likely to have somewhat of a warm time, I think I should feel better satisfied to have a season of prayer."

Albert knit his brow in moody silence. Mary heaved a deep sigh. Mr. Gracelius was called in, and having read the 20th Psalm, he offered up the following prayer:—

"Oh! Thou mighty God of Jacob, who didst accompany Thine ancient Israel through all their trials, and didst fight their battles for them, we thank Thee that Thou hast taught us to put our trust in Thee. And we beseech Thee, oh! blessed Father, for the sake of Thine own Son Jesus Christ, to help us at this time in our endeavor to appropriate to the support of this branch of thy Zion, the treasures which, for the mere purposes of an unhallowed commerce, are being transported to that people who have ever distinguished themselves by their infidelity, and by their scorn of all true religion; who have also by their mighty leaders devastated kingdoms and shed seas of blood to gratify a vain-glorious ambition.

"Oh! Lord, we would not shed blood needlessly, and we therefore pray Thee to enable us in the approaching conflict, to have a single eye to Thy glory, and thus preserve a calm and kind temper, whatsoever may be the resistance offered on this occasion. And wilt Thou, O Lord, assist our beloved captain to do his duty, and to so command his men and order the battle, that when all shall be over, he may have a conscience void of offence towards God and towards man. And whatsoever treasures may come to us, may we gratefully employ in Thy service and to Thy glory, remembering that Jesus Christ, who died for us and rose again for our justification, first became poor, that we through his poverty might be made rich, and therefore that we ought to use our wealth to the advancement of Christianity in our own souls and among our fellow-beings, as the best evidence of our gratitude for our earthly prosperity, and for those treasures which are laid up for us in heaven; and to Thy gracious name, Father, Son, and Holy Spirit, be the praise forever. *Amen.*"

The tone of the chaplain's voice, the fervid manner and the striking pathos of this short prayer, had a strong effect upon Captain Templeton and his wife. They both rose from their knees with tears in their eyes.

The Captain grasped the hand of Mr. Gracelius, and earnestly said: "I feel strengthened, my brother; and I can now say, If the Lord be for us, who can be against us!" He then passed out and resumed his position on the deck.

"Miss St. Clair," said Mrs. Templeton, "do you think that can be wickedness which the Lord sanctifies with his communion?"

Before Mary could reply, the loud report of a cannon gave notice that the action had commenced.

The struggle was a short one, the French vessel was captured, with the loss of her commander, who fell at the first fire. It took but a short time to have all on the merchantman in fetters, and the vessel manned by the pirates.

It was not until the morning after the capture that matters became composed on the pirates' vessel, and everything in usual order.

At breakfast Mary took the liberty to ask the Captain what he designed to do with his prisoners.

"I always endeavor," he replied, "to remember the obligations of humanity and Christianity. Sometimes, for our own safety, we are compelled to put our captives to death, but I do so always with great reluctance, and never without prayer to God that their souls might be saved. In this case I think we shall not be under this painful necessity."

"Captain," said Albert, "it is perfectly unaccountable to me how a man of your naturally humane and benevolent disposition can engage in this business of robbery and murder."

"Well, Mr. Gillon," replied the Captain, "I make every allowance for one who has been educated as you have been, and taught that pirates were only worthy of the gallows; although I cannot but feel that your language is not such as your refined and polished manners would warrant me to expect and require. Our business is not robbery and murder. The laws under which we live, both social and political, are as decidedly opposed to such crimes as among any other people."

"I did not," replied Albert, "intend to be ungentlemanly in my language, and was not aware that these terms were offensive to you. But, sir, you only increase my amazement. I cannot comprehend how you can characterize your business by terms more appropriate. Is it not so that piracy is but the practice of robbery and murder, when it takes away a man's possessions, and then destroys his life to make the booty secure?"

"I perceive, Mr. Gillon, that you labor under the delusion that all pirates are bad and cruel men. I confess, sir, there are many of our people who treat their prisoners with unnecessary severity, and frequently inflict death when the occasion does not demand it. But, my dear sir, this is the abuse of piracy, not its legitimate use."

"And do you really mean to say, Captain Templeton," said Mary, "that piracy can be made an honorable business?"

"Of course I do, miss," replied the Captain, "and I regret that Miss St. Clair can suppose I would engage in a business that I did not believe to be honorable."

"But, Captain, you profess to be a Christian, and it is a great mystery to me how you can reconcile your profession with your practice. Surely you do not believe that the Scriptures justify such a life."

"That is precisely my belief, Miss," replied the Captain. "Piracy is a Bible institution, and if it were not so, I would abandon it at once."

"Ah!" said Albert, "that accounts for it. It is that belief in the Bible that leads the mind and the heart astray from the clear principles of a sound moral philosophy. Even my good Mary, here, is so warped by her reverence for the Bible, that she defends the institution of slavery, which I abhor with all my heart. But, Captain, although I am not surprised at your belief that the Bible sanctions piracy, since it is quoted by Christians in support of all sorts of wickedness, I am surprised that a man of your good sense and keen moral perception in regard to other matters of life, should not perceive that slavery, and piracy, and war, and everything of the sort, are irreconcilable with sound morality."

"I do not know," replied the Captain, "what might be the conclusions of abstract reasoning upon the subject outside of the Bible, for I have never thought very profoundly about it. But I feel satisfied so long as I have the assurance that the revealed Word is on my side."

"But, Captain," said Mary, "I am not willing to allow that the Bible is on your side. It shocks me to hear you say so."

"Well, Miss St. Clair, I must turn you over to brother Gracelius, who is well posted up in Bible matters. He will be able to show you that piracy is a Bible institution."

"Yes, my young sister," said Mr. Gracelius, who had not been inattentive to the conversation, while he was enjoying an excellent cup of coffee. "The Scriptures do most certainly sanction the institution of piracy."

Here Mr. Gracelius took from his pocket a small Bible, and proceeded to say: "On such a question, I am strongly disposed to pass by all ethical and metaphysical dissertation, and appeal at once to the only standard of right and wrong which can prove decisive. It is the responses of the sacred oracles to which we must after all appeal."

"I could wish, Mr. Gracelius," said Albert, "that you would discuss this question rather upon the foundation principles of morality, than by arguments from a volume which sanctions war, slavery, death penalties, and a host of other evils, by the very confessions of Christians themselves."

"I perceive," said Mr. Gracelius, "that you, sir, have never yet learned the true grace of God through regeneration, or you too would bow submissively to the teachings of the sacred Scriptures, and acknowledge them as the highest standard of right and morality. I cannot, therefore, hope to seriously affect your mind by an appeal to the Bible. But Miss St. Clair, being a Christian, will feel the force of such high authority."

"Truly, Mr. Gracelius," said Mary, "I do take the Bible as my highest standard of truth; and it is from the principles taught by the Bible that I have the assurance that piracy is awfully criminal. And I am utterly astonished that a man of your apparent piety, and who so well understands the doctrines of Christianity, can for a moment think that the Bible justifies such crimes."

"My dear young sister," said the minister, "you are begging the question when you call piracy a crime, for that is the very thing you are to prove. But let us see what piracy is:

"In order to clear away rubbish, and to arrive at once at the point, let me remind you that it is simply the *essential* character of piracy which we are discussing. Piracy itself is nothing more than the appropriating of the products of another's labor and skill, without his consent or contract. The absence of the contract, or the consent of the producer, does not alter the nature and extent of the pirates' right. The case is analogous to that of parents and children. A father has a right to the productions of his child's labor during his minority, without the contract or consent of the child, and he may even transfer that right. But I grant that this does not justify the father in doing anything to the detriment of the child, either morally, intellectually, or physically. And, beyond doubt, this is the true light in which Christianity would have pirates regard their relations. The capture of a vessel, and the treatment of prisoners, involve a great responsibility. Nothing more should be done than is absolutely essential to the maintenance of the peculiar institutions of piracy. It is not the relation of the pirate to the producer or prisoner which is sinful, but infidelity to the solemn trust which that relation creates. It does not follow, because he has a right to the produce of another's labor or skill, that he has also a right to inflict unnecessary violence on his person, or take from him all means of livelihood. Whenever it can be done, without jeopardizing the well-being and interests of our society and institutions, we ought to spare the prisoner's life, make him comfortable while in our hands, place him as soon as possible where he can return to his home, and leave him means enough to keep him from starving or absolute destitution.

"To include in the idea of piracy, that also of robbery and murder, is to confound two things entirely distinct, and which really have no sort of connection. If I take from another that which I have no right to by the laws of the society or government under which I live, then I am a robber; for that alone is property which the law makes property, as one of your own great statesmen has very properly said; and if I take life, when not essential to maintain my own rights under the laws of that government which I recognize in my social obligations, I am a murderer. I therefore insist upon it, that, in discussing this subject, we regard as appropriate to the question only the *essential* elements of piracy, and not its abuses; for piracy may exist without inflicting these aggravated wrongs.

"Christian pirates have great regard for the welfare, temporal and spiritual, of their fellow-beings, and oftentimes exercise the spirit of the most self-denying missionaries. Such men and women do honor to human nature. They are the true friends of their race.

"Now, here is piracy—a system of society and government which gives opportunity to inculcate among graceless men who fall into our hands the principles of the Gospel of Christ; and many an ungodly man has had the opportunity in our cabin of hearing the doctrines of the cross, who, whilst immersed in the business, and cares, and pleasures of life, never darkened the door of a meeting-house on land. And many of them have been converted to the Christian faith, and have become excellent and worthy Christian pirates.

"Those of our captains who have Christian sailors under them have the best-managed vessels; and really their crews do more of effective work, both in battle and in ship duties, than any ungodly crew that can be found.

"No, Sister Mary, depend upon it, you have imbibed a prejudice against piracy, and you suppose it to involve all sorts of crime. But the true question of issue between us is pruned to this:—Is it necessarily a crime in the sight of God to control the property, or curtail the personal liberty, or take the life of a human being in any case?

"Every government has necessarily a right to pass laws indispensable to its existence; and it has a right, also, to establish those regulations which shall best promote the good of the whole population. Now, what political organization is most desirable for a particular people, depends on circumstances; but, whatever be that adopted, whether democracy, or despotism, or piratical confederation, the rights of man, as a human being, are trenched upon; and visionary have proved and will prove all projects of constructing and fashioning society according to philosophical notions and theories of abstract unalienable rights. That piracy or any civil institution interferes with the property of a man, or a class of men (as, for instance, merchants), does not then make it necessarily, and, amid all circumstances, a crime."

Mr. Gracelius here paused, and gave Mary an opportunity to put in a word.

"But," said she, "after taking off what you call the rubbish, Mr. Gracelius, and pruning the question down as much as you please, I cannot possibly admit that the Bible anywhere justifies piracy under any circumstances whatsoever, either abstractly or practically. I call upon you for anything in all the Bible that gives the slightest countenance to such a mode of life, or such a government, as you are pleased to term it."

"I should rather require of you," replied the learned divine, "to make out from the Bible your charge that piracy is a crime. I know not a word from the first of Genesis to the end of Revelation where piracy is once condemned. But I pass this, and, waiving my clear logical rights, undertake to prove the negative, and to show that the Bible does, most explicitly, both by precept and example, bear me out in my assertion, that piracy is not necessarily, and always, and amidst all circumstances, a sin. WHAT GOD SANCTIONED IN THE OLD TESTAMENT, AND PERMITTED IN THE NEW, CANNOT BE SIN.

"I begin with the patriarch Jacob, whose name

Israel has been appropriated from his day to this time to the true church. How did Jacob acquire his great riches? Was it not by appropriating the property of Laban to himself? And did not God bless him in thus doing? There is not a word of condemnation; but, on the contrary, Jacob, in telling his brother that he had much property, remarked, that God had dealt graciously with him. Here, you see, is a marked case of an appropriation of another's property by a very adroit stratagem, which is fully justified by the Old Testament, and uncondemned by the New.

"Had Jacob not represented in his person a different community from Laban's, of which he was to be the Patriarch, his mode of acquiring wealth out of Laban would have been censurable. But his conduct towards Laban was consistent with what was subsequently allowed under the Mosaic laws on the part of the Jews towards other nations. They could, for instance, make slaves of the nations round about;—they could take usury of them;—they could despoil them by war, and they could do a variety of things in relation to the people of other nations which would have been robbery, fraud, murder, and so on, if done by Jews to Jews. Thus the idea that that is property which the law makes property, is of divine origin.

"Take now the case of the Israelites in their exodus from Egypt; they were positively enjoined by the Divine command to borrow of their Egyptian neighbors their various costly jeweleries, not with the idea of returning them, but of appropriating them permanently to their own benefit.

"David, who was a man after God's own heart, did not regard it robbery to obtain from the Priest the shew-bread itself, although to do so he deceived the Priest by telling that which, under other circumstances, would be called a lie. It was essential to his life—to his support. It was not therefore criminal to tell the falsehood in order to obtain the bread. Now, it is upon this very principle that your government and all civil governments employ diplomatic agents, in order to secure by adroitness and craftiness commercial and other advantages; and it is upon the same principle that we pirates justify our proceedings. It is essential to the support and maintenance of our people; and there is as much in the Scriptures to warrant our stratagems to decoy vessels and get the benefit of their cargoes, as for your government to obtain advantages by diplomatic adroitness. We must have a living.

"But you say we not only rob but murder. But as all appropriations of others' possessions are not essentially robbery, so all killing is not essentially murder. If you will look into the Book of Judges, xiv. 19, you will find that the taking of spoil even by violence and bloodshed, is not necessarily a crime—is not necessarily robbery and murder. It is the case of Samson when he had to give thirty changes of raiment to those who had expounded his riddle. It is said: "And the Spirit of the Lord came upon him, and he went down to Askelon and slew thirty men of them, and took their spoil, and gave change of garments unto them which expounded the riddle." Now, notice this particularly, that Samson did all this under the influence of God's Spirit. And you will remember that Paul in Hebrews mentions Samson with special commendation.

"Now, if Samson, and David, and Jacob did such things, we feel justified in proceeding accordingly.

"But as I have not time to go into very minute detail, I pass at once to two very important points in the New Testament. The first occurs in Christ's parable of the unjust steward. There the steward is commended for making an arrangement by which he secured his permanent interest by adroitly subtracting from what was due his Lord by his debtors. He had acted unjustly in the office of steward, being bound by honor to fulfil its duties and his obligations to his employer, but so soon as his obligations to his employer ceased on being ordered out of the stewardship, and his very living cut off, then it was no longer unjust, but commendable to do that which before would have been fraud or robbery.

"The other case is that of our blessed Lord himself. He sent his disciples to take away from the place where they were tied an ass and her colt; and he told them how to escape should they be caught at it, by saying: 'The Lord hath need of them.' Now, when we take away the property of others, we may reply to those who question us, 'The Lord hath need of them,' for every good pirate will endeavor so to use what he obtains as to promote the best interests of religion, and to glorify our blessed Redeemer.

"And now, my dear young sister, what more need I say to establish the point that piracy is not essentially sinful—that it is not *malum in se?* Indeed, it stands upon the same footing that slavery does, and is vindicated by the same process of reasoning. The argument for slavery is identically the same in principle as for piracy. And you know it is upon the ground that slavery is not under all circumstances a sin, that Christians in the Northern States hold communion with you of the South. And I admire that charitable spirit which induces them to believe that Southern Christians do not uphold the barbarous features which wicked and cruel masters impress upon the system of slavery. They give you, therefore, very properly, the right hand of Christian fellowship, which they could not do if slaveholding were sin in itself. And I doubt not they would as readily commune with Christian pirates, since it is evident that piracy is not, any more than slavery, *malum in se.*"

Mary made no reply, but sat musing with a countenance overwhelmed with sadness.

Mr. Gracclius looked as though he had accomplished a decided victory; and Captain Templeton smiled with approbation.

Albert after a short silence exclaimed with great emphasis: "I thank God *my* Bible is my *reason*, my *conscience*, and my *heart*. I this day glory in being an infidel."

"Oh! Albert, Albert!" cried Mary, and burst into tears.

Albert seeing he had wounded the feelings of one he loved so dearly, tried to soothe her by remarking that he had met at the North with some persons who maintained that the Bible was misunderstood and misinterpreted by the most of the commentators and theologians, and that when rightly explained and received, would be found to be perfectly in harmony with the sympathies and philanthropic emotions of the human heart, and with the principles of enlightened reason. But as these persons were generally called fanatical and visionary, he had not paid much attention to their strictures. "I intend, however," he added, "to take an early opportunity to investigate the Bible for myself, and if it prove itself to be better than its commentators and expounders, perhaps I shall become a Christian. But I cannot be a Christian if Christianity props up slaveholding and piracy."

Here the conversation was interrupted by the entrance of a messenger, who announced that every preparation had been made, and that Mr. Gillon and

Miss St. Clair could now go on board the merchant vessel. On rising to depart, Albert with much feeling addressed the Captain:

"Captain Templeton, we are much indebted to you for saving our lives, and for the hospitality and very kind attentions we have received. I would that I could repay you in some way. But you will pardon me, so young a man, for expressing the profound wish of my heart, that you would abandon this horrible life, and no longer delude yourself with the idea that the Bible is the highest authority for the regulation of man's life. Recognize every man, everywhere, as your brother, and treat all as you have treated Mary and myself,—treat all as your own heart, left to its most benevolent promptings, would dictate, and (the Bible to the contrary notwithstanding) you will please God better than you can do by any adherence to theological dogmas, that make the Almighty the author of piracy, slavery, war, death-penalties, and such like institutions and practices."

"And I, too, hope," replied Captain Templeton, "that you will look into this matter with care, and come to the conclusion to follow that good book rather than the *ignis fatuus* of mere human reason and natural conscience. I admire your honesty and candor, Mr. Gillon, and, although I cannot but regard your views as fanatical, I trust that when the ardor of youth shall give place to the reflections of maturer years, you will be as firm a believer in the Bible as I am."

"Ah!" said Mr. Gracelius, "that will depend upon the grace of God. Farewell, young man, and may the Lord convert your soul and give us a happy meeting again, where we shall sing the song of the Lamb forever and ever."

Mary, still in tears, took Mr. Gracelius by the hand and said:

"Mr. Gracelius, I am not at all convinced that the Scriptures favor your views, although I am not prepared to meet your arguments. But I fear you have so confirmed Albert in his infidelity, that it will be exceedingly hard to get him hereafter even to listen to Christian instruction."

"Oh! my young sister," replied the minister, "the grace of God can conquer the worst of infidels, and I hope your friend will yet become an ambassador of Christ."

By this time the party were standing on deck, ready

to bid the last adieu. Our young friends were soon on board the merchant vessel and out of sight of their strange benefactors.

They found that the pirates had liberated the crew and passengers, and returned them to their vessel, retaining only the rich cargo.

Having been well supplied with funds, in gold, when they left home, which Albert had about his person when taken up by the pirates, they found no difficulty, on reaching France, in making their way to England, and thence to the United States.

On the voyages Albert perused the Scriptures with great attention, not only because Mary had urged him to do so, but because he felt that he needed to be informed of the true nature and character of what was claimed to be sacred writings. He was careful to avoid conversation on the subject during the progress of his investigations; and Mary herself was not, after her last interview with Mr. Gracelius, sufficiently quieted in her own mind to give expression to her thoughts.

It was in November, when an Indian summer was augmenting the beauty of the scenery about the harbor of New York, that our young friends were sitting together in Mary's spacious state-room on board the noble vessel which was just passing Staten Island.

"Albert," said Mary, with deep emotion, and the tear in her eye, "I have become an Abolitionist."

"And I," said Albert, with yet deeper emphasis, "have become a Christian."

"Thank God—thank God!" exclaimed Mary. "O, Albert, I cannot tell you how happy I am to hear you say so. But I do not need any explanation, for I see through it all. The pirates have made me an Abolitionist, and the Bible has made you a Christian. I have now learned how to understand its teachings, and you have learned that the precious volume has been grievously tortured to uphold the evil instead of the good."

"It is even so, Mary," replied Albert. "I have been reading and studying with an earnest desire for truth. I find much, in the Old Testament, calculated to bewilder, and much that requires the New Testament to explain. I find, scattered through the Old Testament, holy principles that are brought into full relief by Jesus Christ, who has, by his example, and in his instructions to his disciples, elucidated what was obscure and rejected from the claims of divine authority what was only Jewish misconception. I am satisfied that it does not uphold violence, oppression, and wrong, and throw around these things the sanction of the divine mind. I find that everything taught by Jesus Christ is in full harmony with the most benevolent and honorable feelings of the human heart, and with the highest sense of justice and consciousness of right, and is diametrically opposed to all base carnal passions and affections, and to all that is violative of human equality and brotherhood.

"I believe in Jesus Christ. And I had the ideal of such a Saviour for man before I saw that the Jesus of the New Testament is the true Captain of Salvation. And now I find that such a Saviour really exists, I am willing to follow his leadings, although I know it will require self-denials and sacrifices. I tell you, Mary, I found out from reading the Bible that I was an unregenerated man, and needed God's spirit to purify and sanctify my heart; and I have learned this from studying carefully the life and doctrines of Christ, who, in the flesh, gave a full manifestation of the godhead, and by *his righteousness* brought to my own view *my unrighteousness*.

"I read of Jesus dying on the cross rather than not

carry out every jot and every tittle of the divine morality, and every principle of pure and undefiled religion. I stand in admiration of this divine heroism. I learn farther that his great mission was to induce sinful man to abandon his sins and become reconciled to God; and that it was in carrying out this mission that he subjected himself to the tortures of the cross. Under the influence of God's Spirit, this brings me to true repentance, and I determine to reform by taking Jesus as my exemplar and the captain of my salvation. I am thus made reconciled to God's law, and feel pardoned for the past and hopeful for the future. My faith in Christ gives me strength to live the life of a Christian, and thus I am saved. Jesus Christ's death has in this way reconciled me to God, and being thereby brought into harmony with God, God is reconciled to me. Jesus Christ therefore making atonement or reconciliation for me, has truly suffered in my stead. That is to say, his suffering in order to impress me with my obligations to God and his law, has by reconciling me to God's law, kept me from suffering the penalty of law. And when I think that God made this provision for this fallen world—that he gave his only begotten Son, that whosoever believeth in him should not perish but have eternal life, and I realize it all with trust and confidence, I feel that the kingdom of heaven is within me. I am truly happy."

"My dear Albert," responded Mary, "you make me to see all this in a new light. I confess I never before properly understood the doctrine of the atonement. I did not before understand that atonement for man, and reconciliation between God and man, were one and the same thing. But I now perceive that there is no atonement unless we become Christ-like; and that just in proportion as we are Christ-like, we are in harmony with God, and are thus far saved. God converts the soul from the love of sin to the love of Christ, and that love of Christ insures obedience to his commandments to the full measure of our knowledge. To be clothed upon then with the righteousness of Christ, and to have Christ's righteousness imputed to us, are not terms signifying a righteousness extraneous from ourselves, and only regarded in place of righteousness in us, but really and truly to manifest a righteousness which will be seen and recognized by our ownselves and others as a righteousness derived from Christ, because we live as Christ would have us to live. O how pleasant it is to see the matter in so clear a light!"

"And now," said Albert, "I wish to know how it is you a little while ago called yourself an Abolitionist. Did you really mean what you said in its full import?"

"Yes I did," replied Mary. "That argument made by Mr. Gracelius was so exactly similar to the mode of interpreting the Scriptures in behalf of slavery, that I at once saw if it were good for slavery, it was just as good in defence of piracy; and that I must give up the Bible under such a mode of interpretation, or admit that piracy itself is sanctioned by the Bible. I could not give up my precious Bible, for I have felt so much of its hallowed influences upon my soul, that I could not think of parting from it. I have, like yourself, spent this voyage studying it with great care, and whatever may be the criticisms of the learned upon words, I am certain that the whole spirit of Christianity, as developed before and since Christ, utterly condemns any and every system, or practice, or principle which does not recognize all men as brethren. And I also perceive that many things have been wrested from their original meaning to subserve the purposes of oppression and tyranny. I now so read that good book, that I discriminate between the erroneous ideas and practices of the Jews and the divine law—between historical facts and traditional inferences—between man's misconceptions and the true principles of religion. I now can and do see from the Bible itself that slavery is all wrong; and being so, I am obliged to be an Abolitionist; for I know that no Christian ought to continue the practice of what is wrong in itself on any consideration. But, Albert, how was it that you who did not believe in the Bible, became an Abolitionist?"

"Why, Mary, the truth is, I did not believe in the Bible, because, being an Abolitionist, professed Christians and ministers instructed me that the Bible sanctioned slavery, and that it required obedience to earthly masters and rulers, even although their commands and laws be contrary to the divine law. This was so contrary to my sense of natural right, that I said to myself I cannot honor the true God by submitting to the authority of the Bible; and therefore it was I took an utter aversion to the Bible. My respect for my parents prevented me from telling them when they would urge me to read the Bible, that their own views and practice had already convinced me that it was an unrighteous book; for I could not believe that my father would hold slaves under any conviction of its rightfulness drawn from nature, and that my mother would treat the blacks as she did, had she been governed by her natural sense of justice; but that by early education in the Bible, they had been trained to regard slaveholding perfectly compatible with the divine law, and the black as some heathenish being, whom it was no oppression to enslave. But now having examined the Bible with care, I see that they who take that Book to justify the enslaving of men, have been most dreadfully deluded."

"Well, Albert," said Mary, "you know the obligations of Christianity require action as well as sentiment. If we are Christians truly, we have to serve Christ fully. We dare not, therefore, withhold our testimony against slavery any more than against any other crime. How then can we return to Carolina? We cannot be happy there amidst an institution which we abhor."

"Mary, like yourself, I now feel," said Albert, "that a Christian must not hide his light under a bushel. We must speak for the dumb and for the truth as it is in Jesus. But with such views and intentions we would not be suffered in South Carolina. What, then, are we to do?"

Mary, after a few moments' meditation, answered, "Albert, our parents think we were lost with the Pulaski. Let it stand so. They will suffer more if we go back to them with such sentiments as we now entertain. And for your sake, and for our parents' sake, and for the sake of Christ, I am willing to sacrifice all my worldly prospects and try to make a living by my own exertions in some place where my own feelings will not be shocked with the perpetual violation of Christian law by my own slaveholding relatives, and where I shall not be myself an annoyance to them."

Here their dialogue was interrupted by the arrival of the ship at the wharf, and in a short time our young friends were safely landed in New York.

Suffice it to say, in conclusion, that they both agreed never more to be dependent on the wealth of their parents,—assured as they were that all they could bestow upon them would be the product of unrequited toil. They were soon united in holy wedlock, and, after engaging in teaching an academy a short time, Albert became a faithful and zealous minister of the gospel; and he and his loving wife in process of time succeeded in revealing their situation to their parents, in such terms as to reconcile them to their anti-slavery views, and to induce them finally to emancipate their slaves.

They are all living happily in moderate circumstances, in a little town in one of the free States,—in the direct line of the "under-ground railroad;" and many a poor fugitive finds a comfortable shelter in either of their humble cottages.

A short time since, Mary was reading the discussion between Dr. Wayland and Dr. Fuller, on the subject of slavery, and was startled to find the very words of Mr. Gracelius and his identical argument, used by the champion of American slavery.

"Albert," said she to her husband, "would you believe it, Dr. Fuller and Mr. Gracelius are one and the same person."

"It surely cannot be!" said Albert. But to this day the matter looks very mysterious to them. And it is hoped that Dr. Fuller or Dr. Wayland will explain the coincidence of the arguments in some satisfactory manner.

Wm Henry Brisbane

Toil and Trust.

THIS is the motto of all persons sincerely disposed to embrace the cross of the anti-slavery enterprise. The duty it imposes is two-fold; 1. To *toil* for the spread of the truth; and 2. To *trust* to the dissipation of error. The most potent barrier set up against the opponents of slavery is made of the prejudices carefully instilled into the popular mind against them. I propose, in brief, to point out their origin.

It is sedulously inculcated:

1. That anti-slavery is a pure sectional feeling, and springs from jealousy of the South.

Fifty years ago this idea might fairly have been entertained. Many of the arguments then used have no better root than political jealousy. But it is not so now. The ruling objection at present is, that slavery is WRONG, no matter where it may be found; that it is a moral evil, and an offence against religion, not less than a great political curse; that indifference to it among good men encourages its extension among bad men; and that nothing but resolute and universal condemnation of it in every form will stimulate to its abolition. How far these views are from jealousy of the South, must appear obvious enough to all who reflect that those who entertain them, consider the result to be arrived at as one which must spring from the voluntary convictions of those most affected by it, that they are getting rid of the only serious drawback to their own prosperity. Of course, then, it is the best interests of the South,—their strength, moral, social, and political,—that anti-slavery men believe they are promoting, by their course.

2. That the enemies of slavery desire to subvert the Constitution and to dissolve the Union.

Possibly, a few impatient spirits may have got so far. They constitute, however, but a very small portion of the number included in the term. Nine-tenths of these hold that neither the Constitution nor the Union should be brought into question at all. They consider that the resort to them as a protection and safeguard to slavery, by ill-judging and rash conservatives, has done more to put them into serious danger, than the acts of all others combined during the present century. Any man who relies upon a good government to sustain acknowledged evil, does much to modify the notions of goodness which honest and conscientious men have entertained respecting that government. He furnishes an entering wedge for doubt and distrust, which, if not removed, will grow into aversion. Anti-slavery men reason differently. They separate slavery from the Constitution and the Union, and, by seeking to destroy the former, desire to perpetuate the latter. They hold, that against the concentrated moral sentiment of the whole country, acting through its legitimate public channels, and aided by the prayers and the hopes of all the civilized world, it would be much more difficult to maintain slavery in the States, than if the dangers of general misgovernment and disunion were to come in to distract the public attention, and open up social disasters of a worse kind than those which they seek to remedy.

3. The spirit of this reform is denunciatory, violent, and proscriptive.

It is inevitable that all movements directed against

the established errors of communities originate with men more or less fanatical in spirit. None but they have the necessary elements of character to advance at all. But, as others become convinced of the fundamental truths which they utter, the tendency of their association is to modify and soften the tone, and make it more nearly approximate the correct sentiment. At this period, there is quite as much of liberality among anti-slavery men as is consistent with a determined maintenance of their general purpose. Though disposed to be just to all who conscientiously differ with them in opinion, they cannot overlook the fact that many honest persons are too indifferent, and more are too compromising in their views of slavery. To rouse the one, and alarm the other class into a conviction of their responsibility for their apathy, is one of the most imperative duties. It may be that this is not always done in the most courtly or the choicest terms. Some allowances must be made for the spirit of liberty. These cases form, however, the exception, and not the rule, among anti-slavery men. The great majority well comprehend that the greatest results will follow efforts made without bitterness of temper. They remember that whilst the Saviour denounced without stint the formal scribe, the hollow Pharisee, and the greedy money-changer, he chose for his sphere of exertion the society of publicans and sinners.

4. Anti-slavery men seek to set slaves against their masters, at the risk of the lives and happiness of both.

This impression, which is much the most common, is, at the same time, the least founded in truth of all. No evidence, worthy of a moment's credit, has ever been produced, implicating any class of them in a suspicion of the kind. Nothing proves the absence of all malignity towards the slaveholders more clearly than this. If they sought really to injure them, what could be more easy than to stimulate disaffection along so extensive a line of boundary as that of the slave States? Probably few of them entertain any doubt of the abstract *right* of the slave to free himself from the condition in which he is kept against his own consent, in any manner practicable. How easy then the step from this opinion to an act of encouragement! That it has never been taken furnishes the most conclusive proof of the falsity of the popular impression, and of the moderations of the anti-slavery men, who seek only, in the moral convictions of the masters, for the source of freedom to the slaves.

But though it be true that all these common impressions are delusions strewn in the way of anti-slavery men to impair the effect of their exertions, it by no means follows that they should be induced by them to assume a moderation which encourages sluggishness. No great movement in human affairs can be made without zeal, energy, and perseverance. It must be animated by a strong will, and tempered by a benevolent purpose. Such is the shape which the anti-slavery reform is gradually assuming. Its motto, then, should be, as was said in the beginning:

"TOIL AND TRUST."

Charles Francis Adams.

QUINCY, 10 July, 1853.

Friendship for the Slave is Friendship for the Master.

IT is a mistake on the part of the people of the south to suppose that those who desire the extinction of slavery, whether residing in America or England, are actuated by unfriendly feelings toward them personally, or by any hostility to the pecuniary or social interests of their section of country. The most important and influential classes of the population, both of England and of the northern States of this Union, have a direct and strong pecuniary interest at stake, in the prosperity and welfare of the south. If the people of Massachusetts or those of Lancashire were employed in raising cotton and sugar, and if the prices which they obtained for their produce were kept down by southern competition, then there might perhaps be some ground for suspecting a covert hostility in any action or influence which they might attempt to exert on such a question. But the contrary is the fact. New England and Old England manufacture and consume the cotton and sugar which the south produces. They are directly and deeply interested in having the production of these articles go on in the most advantageous manner possible. The southern planter is not their competitor and rival. He is their partner. His work is to them and to their pursuits one of co-operation and aid. Consequently his prosperity is their prosperity, and his ruin would be an irretrievable disaster, not a benefit, to them. They are thus naturally his friends, and, consequently, when in desiring a change in the relation which subsists between him and his laborers, they declare that they are not actuated by any unfriendly feeling toward him, but honestly think that the change would be beneficial to all concerned, there is every reason why they should be believed.

There was a time when the laboring population of England occupied a position in respect to the proprietors of the soil there, very analogous to that now held by African slaves in our country. But the system has been changed. From being serfs, compelled to toil for masters, under the influence of compulsion or fear, they have become a free peasantry, working in the employment of landlords, for wages. But this change has not depressed or degraded the landlords, or injured them in any way. On the contrary, it has probably elevated and improved the condition of the master quite as much as it has that of the man.

Imagine such a change as this on any southern plantation: the Christian master desiring conscientiously to obey the divine command,—given expressly for his guidance, in his responsible relation of employer,—that he should "give unto his servants that which is just and equal,—forbearing threatening,"—resolves that he will henceforth induce industry on his estate by the payment of honest wages, instead of coercing his laborers by menaces and stripes; and after carefully considering the whole ground, he estimates, as fairly and faithfully as he can, what proportion of the whole avails of his culture properly belong to the labor performed by his men, and what to the capital, skill, and supervision, furnished and exercised by himself,—and then fixes upon a rate of wages, graduating the scale fairly and honestly according to the strength, the diligence, and the fidelity of the various laborers. Suppose, also, that some suitable arrangement is made on the plantation or in the vicinity, by which the servants can expend what they earn, in such comforts, ornaments, or luxuries as are adapted to their condition and their ideas. Suppose that, in consequence of the operation of this system, the laborers, instead of desiring, as now, to make their escape from the scene of labor, should each prize and value his place in it, and fear dismission from it as a punishment. Suppose that through the change which this new state of things should produce, it should become an agreeable and honorable duty to superintend and manage the system, as it is now agreeable and honorable to superintend the operations of a manufactory, or the construction or working of a railway, or the building of a fortress, or any other organized system of industry where the workmen are paid, and that consequently, instead of rude and degraded overseers, intemperate and profane, extorting labor by threats and severity, there should be found a class of intelligent, humane, and honest men, to direct and superintend the industry of the estate,—men whom the proprietor would not be ashamed to associate with, or to admit to his parlor or table. In a word, suppose that the general contentment and happiness which the new system would induce in all concerned in it, were such that peace of mind should return to the master's breast, now,—especially in hours of sickness and suffering, and at the approach of death,—so often disturbed, and a sense of safety be restored to his family, so that it should no longer be necessary to keep the pistols or the rifle always at hand, and that the wife and children could lie down and sleep at night, without starting at unusual or sudden sounds, or apprehending insurrection when they hear the cry of fire. Suppose that such a change as this were possible, is it the part of a friend or an enemy to desire to have it effected?

But all such suppositions as these, the southern man will perhaps say, are visionary and utopian in the highest degree. No such state of things as is contemplated by them, can by any possibility be realized with such a population as the southern slaves. Very well; say *this*, if you please, and prove it, if it can be proved. But do not charge those who desire that it might be realized, with being actuated, in advocating the change, by unfriendly feelings towards you,—for most assuredly they do not entertain any.

Jacob Abbott.

Christine.

"O, these childen, how they do lie round our hearts."—MILLY EDMONDSON.

THE clock struck the appointed hour, and the sale commenced. Articles of household furniture, horses, carts, and slaves, were waiting together to be sold to the highest bidder. For strange as it would seem in another land than this, beneath the ample folds of the "Star-spangled Banner," *human sinews* were to be bought and sold. Bodies, such as the Apostle called the "temples of the Holy Ghost," in which dwelt souls for which Christ died;—men, women and little children, made in the image of God, were classed with marketable commodities, to be sold by the pound, like dumb beasts in the shambles. Husbands would be torn from their wives, mothers from their children, and *all* from everything they loved most dearly.

The group of *human chattels* excited great interest among the lookers-on, for they were a choice lot of prime negroes, and rumor said that he would get a rare bargain who bought that day.

It was a saddening sight, that dusky group, whose only crime was being

"—— guilty of a skin
Not colored like our own,"

as they waited with anxious looks and quivering hearts to hear their doom, filling up the dreary moments with thoughts of the chances and changes which overhung their future.

A bright-eyed boy, of twelve years old,

"A brave, free-hearted, careless one,"

with a proud spirit playing in every line of his handsome face, and in every movement of his graceful form, was first called to the auction-block. His good qualities were rapidly enumerated, his limbs rudely examined, his soundness vouched for, and he became the chattel personal of a Georgian, who boasted of his good bargain; and on being warned that he would have trouble with the boy, declared with an oath, that he would "soon take the devil out of him."

Matty, a sister of this lad, was next placed upon the stand. Her beauty, which the excitement of that dreadful moment only served to heighten, hushed for awhile the coarse jests of the crowd. She was a splendid-looking creature, just entering upon womanhood. But her beauty proved, as beauty must ever prove to a slave woman, a deadly curse. It enhanced her market value, and sealed her deadly fate. It attracted the eye, and inflamed the passions of a wealthy Louisianian, named St. Laurent, who gave a thousand dollars in hard gold in exchange for her, that he might make her his petted favorite. Wives, mothers, daughters of America, have *you* nothing to do with slavery, when such is the fate of slave women? *Can* you sit silent, and at your ease, knowing that such things are?

When Matty was removed from the auction-block, she fell upon her brother's neck, and wept such tears as only they can weep whom slavery parts, never to meet again.

"Christine!" cried the loud voice of the auctioneer. Matty checked her passionate grief, and turning saw her mother, with her baby in her arms, standing where she herself had stood but just before. Quickly her keen eye sought the form of her new master. With a sudden impulse she threw herself at his feet, exclaiming, "O master, master, *do* buy my mother too!" The man gazed for a moment on the beautiful face upturned to his, with a look which made the lashes droop over her pleading eyes, and tapping her cheek with his finger, he said,

"What! coaxing so early, my pretty one? No, no; it will not do; I have no use for the old woman."

"Oh, master, she is not old. *Do* buy my mother, master!"

"Here is a prize for you, gentlemen," broke in the harsh tones of the auctioneer. "There is the best housekeeper and cook in all Virginia. Who bids for her? $300 did you say, sir? $325—thanks, gentlemen, but I cannot sell this woman for a song. She is an excellent seamstress. $400—$450—$500—I am glad to see you are warming up a little, gentlemen,—but she is worth more money than that. Look at her! What a form! what an eye! what arms!—there is muscle for you, gentlemen. Upon my honor she is the flower of the lot,—a dark-colored rose,—black, but comely; and her baby goes with her. $550, did I hear you say, sir? Will no one give more than $550 for such a woman and baby?"

"The baby is of no account," said Mr. St. Laurent; "she would sell better without it. If I buy her, I shall give away the little encumbrance."

The poor slave-mother heard him, and strained her baby to her bosom, as if she would say, "You shall *never* take him from me." The boy looked into her face, and smiled a sweet baby smile, and put his little arms about her neck, and laid his cheek on hers. One would have thought he understood what was passing in her heart, and strove to comfort her. "$575—$600—$650,"—and Christine and her baby boy became the property of Mr. St. Laurent.

"I would not have bought the woman," said he, turning to an acquaintance, "but for the girl's importunity. I feared she would have the sulks if I didn't, and I want to keep her good-natured. I shall give the mother as a wedding-present to my daughter. But anybody may have the child, who will take him off my hands?"

"I will take him, sir, and thank you too," said a little, sharp-looking, bustling man, stepping briskly up, and bowing to Mr. St. Laurent.

"Will you, my friend? Then he is yours, and you may take him away as soon as you please."

"If I take him now, the woman will raise a storm," said the little man; "I know a better way than that," and drawing Mr. St. Laurent aside, he communicated his plan, and they parted mutually satisfied.

Meanwhile the sale went on, but we will not follow further its revolting details. Christine, with her baby and Matty, were put in safe quarters for the night. Notwithstanding the intense anxiety that filled their minds, and a superstitious fear in Christine's heart that the worst had not yet come, an unaccountable drowsiness oppressed them, and before long both fell into a deep death-like sleep.

Morning broke over the green earth. The sun gilded the mountain-tops, and bathing the trees in splendor, was greeted with ten thousand bird-songs. He kissed the dewy flowers, and their fragrance rose as incense on the morning air. He looked into the windows of happy homes, and wakened golden-haired children to renew their joyous sports, and mothers, whose

> "—— souls were hushed with their weight of bliss
> Like flowers surcharged with dew,"

sent up their morning thanksgiving to "Him who never slumbers," for His protection of their "laughing dimpled treasures." Suddenly a warm ray fell upon the face of the sleeping slave-mother. She wakened with a start, and with one wild shriek of agony sprang from the bed. Her babe was gone.

Why need we dwell upon what followed? What pen can describe the anguish of the heart-broken mother, when she knew that while under the influence of opiates which she had unwittingly taken, her boy had been taken from her, and that she should look upon her darling's face no more. Mother! look at the darling nestler upon your own bosom, and ask yourself how you would have felt in Christine's place.

After the first burst of agony was over, she did not give way outwardly to grief. One might have thought she did not grieve. But she carried all her sorrows in her heart, till they had eaten out her life.

On the morning of Eleanore St. Laurent's bridal day, Christine was sent for to perform some service for her young mistress. But the spoil had been taken out of the hands of the spoiler—the bruised heart was at rest. The outraged soul had gone with its complaints to the bar of the Eternal.

Anne. P. Adams.

The Intellectual, Moral, and Spiritual Condition of the Slave.

THE American slave is a human being. He possesses all the attributes of mind and heart that belong to the rest of mankind. He has intellect with which to think, sensibility with which to feel, and toil which prompts him to vigorous and manly action. Nor is he destitute of the sublime faculty of reason, which is related to eternal and absolute truths. Imagination and fancy, too, he possesses, in a very large degree. But all these faculties, which nature has bestowed upon the slave in common with other men, by a decree of slavery fixed and unalterable like the laws of the Medes and Persians, are undeveloped, and the results, therefore, of their activities are not to be found. How mean then it must be to reproach the unfortunate slave with a lack of intellectual qualities, such as characterize men generally. In proof of the statement, that slaves have these qualities, it is only necessary to refer to the many fugitives who, by their great thoughts, their masterly logic, and their captivating eloquence, are astonishing both the Old and the New World. Education is what the white man needs for the development of his intellectual energies. And it is what the black man needs for the development of his. Educate him, and his mind proves itself at once as profound and masterly in its conceptions, and as brisk and irresistible in its decisions, as the mind of any other man.

But, in addition to his intellectual, the slave possesses a moral nature, capable of the highest development and the most refined culture. A conscience tender and acute, the voice of God in his soul bidding him to choose the right and avoid the wrong, is his lawful inheritance bestowed upon him by his Heavenly Father. This no one can deny who knows aught of the love of moral truth manifested by the slaves of this country. God has not left the slaves without moral sense. Nor has he denied him the spiritual faculty which, when cultivated, enables him to recognize God in his spiritual manifestations, to discern and appreciate spiritual truths, and to feel and relish the gentle distillations of the spirit of divine love as they fall upon his heart like dew upon the grateful earth. The moral and spiritual nature of the slave, however, like his intellectual, goes uneducated and untrained. Deep, dark, and impenetrable is the gloom which enshrouds the mind and soul of the slave. No ray of light cheers him in his midnight darkness. No one is allowed to fetch him the blessings of education, and no preacher of righteousness is suffered to illumine his dark mind by the presentation of sacred truth.

It is indeed true that slavery is a political, a civil, and a commercial evil. It is true that it is most excruciating and frightful in its effects upon the physical nature of its victim. But slavery is seen in its more awful wickedness and terrible heinousness, when we contemplate the vast waste of intellect, the vast waste of moral and spiritual energy, which has been caused by its poisonous touch.

And yet the power of the State, and the influence of the Church, are given to its support. Many of our leading statesmen are engaged in devising and furthering plans for the extension of its territorial area, thereby hoping to perpetuate and eternize its bloody existence, while the majority of our most distinguished divines find employment in constructing discourses, founded upon perverse expositions of sacred writ, calculated to establish and fix in the minds of the people the impression that slavery is a divine institution.

Although this mighty power of the State, and influence of the Church, be opposed to the slave, let him not despair, but be full of hope. For God is upon his side, truth is upon his side, and a multitude of good and able men and women are engaged in working out his redemption.

J. Mercer Langston

OBERLIN, August 27, 1853.

The Bible vs. Slavery.

"NOTHING," says Dr. Spring, "is more plain to my mind than that the word of God recognizes the relation between master and slave as one of the established institutions of the age; and, that while it addresses slaves as Christian men, and Christian men as slaveholders, it so modifies the whole system of slavery as to give a death-blow to all its abuses, and breathes such a spirit, that in the same proportion in which its principles are imbibed, the yoke of bondage will melt away, all its abuses cease, and every form of human oppression will be unknown. The Bible is no agitator. It changes human governments only as it changes the human character. It aims at transforming the dispositions and hearts of men, and diffusing through all human institutions the supreme love of God, and the impartial love of man."

Now, this either means that the Bible requires that all institutions be adjusted and harmonized with the moral law—the law of love—or it means nothing. For, we maintain, that slavery is *per se* wrong, where the enslaver has no direct warrant from heaven, or the enslaved has not forfeited liberty by crime on principles of recognized and universal equity; and the whole Bible forbidding wrong must be held as forbidding slavery, or any arbitrary and inhuman tamperings with the inalienable rights of a fellow-creature.

If slavery is not a wrong in itself, irrespective of what are called its abuses, then all that is essential in it may be retained from age to age; and all the amelioration which the Christian law superinduces may be such as to consist with the violation of the natural prerogatives of humanity, and with the denial to man of the essential and dearest privileges of social and domestic life, with the denial of the rights of conscience too. For slavery, as distinguished from service by contract, is this thing and no other:—it is labor undefined, unrewarded, on the condition of being used as vendible property, and every independent right of the slave, as an intellectual and moral being, is ignored. By practical indulgence such rights may be sometimes conceded. But the slave-law ceases as such when these are recognized.

Now, we hold it a libel on the Bible to affirm that it sanctions such slavery. We must warn you of the fallacy that lies in this distinction of the thing itself, and its abuse. What is called the abuse here is the essence and the characteristic of the subject. Service as well as slavery may be abused. Everything may be abused. But, the claim of the slaveholder is itself the abuse of the God-ordained relation of master and servant. Can men be regarded as a chattel?—that is the question—and so regarded without his consent, and his family treated as such permanently, without his consent, or even with it?

It comes of this bad interpretation of the Christian law, that in the nineteenth century slavery still remains,—is cherished. It is not that the principles of Christianity do not tend to extinguish it. But men, forcing their false interpretation on the Scriptures, plead their authority for a system or institution, to which their whole spirit is opposed,—and which confesses its unscriptural character by keeping out Christian light, and forbidding the Scriptures with the slave.

To talk of the spirit of Christianity, in distinction from its express or implied law against slavery, is as if one would trust for the extinction of sin against the sixth or seventh commands of the decalogue, by general inculcation of meekness or purity, without denouncing murder and defining it, or defining between allowed and disallowed affinity in the marriage law. We may if we do not proscribe theft, and bring the positive law of God to bear against it, and bring a law into harmony with the divine, be understood, while we talk only of the abuses of property, as warning rather against spending stolen goods in a bad way, than against theft itself? But the design of the moral law is to define rights, as well as to govern the use of them; and it requires that not only the tempers of men, but the institutions of society, be adjusted by the law of equity and charity. It forbids not only the abuse of just power, but all false usurpations of power, and classes man-stealers and extortioners as murderers.

Who, if he but examines the laws of social and rela tive duty, as laid down in the New Testament Epistles, may not discern that the relation of master and servant is recognized side by side with the permanent relations of parent and child, husband and wife, which rest on the law of nature; just because it is not the temporary, unnatural, and violent relation of slaveholder and slave which is recognized, but that of master and servant by contract. The other, its very apologists allow, will pass away; but these duties are enhanced in a law of permanent application, and rest on natural principles, common to all times and all nations.

Mich! Willis

"The Work Goes Bravely on."

LIKE all Reforms which have for their object the amelioration of man's condition; the advancement of the Redeemer's kingdom; the cause of human freedom has encountered many oppositions calculated to impede its progress. It has temporarily suffered from cruel defection within, and the most virulent persecution without the camp.

John, the forerunner of Jesus, had for his portion "locusts and wild honey." But those who have stood forth in the sunlight, the advocates of the crushed and bleeding bondman; whose motto is, "Our country is the world, and our countrymen all mankind," have had no *honey* for *their* portion. Oh no! they have ever dwelt among the tempest and the storm, with thunder, lightning, and whirlwind, to feed upon.

Some have been called, for the advocacy of the

truth, to wing their flight from the prison-house to Heaven; and others, to bare their bosoms to the red-hot indignation of relentless mobs, arrayed in murderous panoply. They have gone; but, thank God, "THE WORK GOES BRAVELY ON!"

The great men of the nation, the mighty men, the chief priests and rulers, have risen in their strength, and resolved to crush, as with an avalanche, the irrepressible aspirations of the bondman's heart for FREEDOM; they have attempted to padlock the out-gushing sympathies of humanity; to trample in the dust the sacred guarantees of the palladium of their own liberties, but their "terribleness hath deceived them, and the pride of their heart," for the desolating angel hath sealed *their* lips in the silence of the tomb, and we, the recipients of their crushing cruelties, thank God "THE WORK GOES BRAVELY ON."

Wm. James Watkins

Slaveholding not a Misfortune but a Crime.

LONDON, September 2, 1853.

"FOR your movement on behalf of the slave, I have profound respect. I assure you of my unfeigned sympathies and of my earnest prayers. In my view, you deserve the high esteem of all who love and serve God. Nothing would be deemed by me a greater honor than co-operation with you actively in your work of faith and your labor of love. With full consent of all that is within me, do I range myself among those who deem American slavery not a sad misfortune, but a heinous crime: a crime all the more heinous, because justified and even perpetrated by men who call themselves the servants of Christ.

"I am, madam, yours respectfully,

William Brock

The Frugality of Slaveholding.

THERE is nothing in the universe that can deserve the name or do the work of valid LAW but the commandment and the ordinance of the living God. All human enactments, adjudications and usages not founded on these, are of no legal force, and should be trampled under foot. The practice of slaveholding, for this reason, can never be legalized, and all legislative or judicial attempts to sustain it are rebellion against God, and treason against civil society. To teach otherwise, would be to set up other gods above Jehovah, to promulgate the fundamental principle of atheism, and proclaim war against the liberties of mankind.

Wm. Goodell

"Ore Perennius."

I ASK no prouder inscription for my humble tomb, than "Here lies the Friend of the Oppressed."

David Paul Brown
Sept 28. 1859

The Mission of America.

Brunswick, Maine, September 30, 1853.

Miss Julia Griffith,

MY Dear Madam, your letter of September 23d I have received. I regret exceedingly that it is not in my power to furnish the article you have done me the honor to solicit, for the "Autographs for Freedom." Particularly do I regret this now, when the great conflict between aristocracy and democracy is about being renewed all over the continent of Europe, and when despots are pointing with exultation to the unparalleled enormities of our "peculiar institutions," and the friends of republican equality, in all lands, are disheartened by our example. Would the slaveholders of the south but consent to place those who till their lands, under the protection of wholesome and impartial law, and pay them honest wages, it would ere long cause human rights to be respected in every corner of the globe. It should be the mission of America, by the silent influence of a glorious example, to revolutionize all despotisms. We have a vast continent to subdue and to adorn, and we need the aid of millions more of willing hands to accomplish the magnificent enterprise. With much esteem I am truly yours,

John S. C. Abbott,

Lewis Tappan

Disfellowshipping Slaveholders.

THE late Dr. Chalmers, not long before his death, spoke with disapprobation of Abolitionists in the United States, "for undertaking," as he said, "to decide, without sufficient evidence, upon the irreligious character of ministers and church-members. *They*, forsooth, undertake to exclude men from the Lord's table, who are in good and regular standing in the church of Christ, because they happen to hold slaves! *They* pretend to decide who, and who are not Christians!" It is marvellous that so learned and so distinguished a man should have fallen into such a mistake; and, on hearsay, ventured to utter a most calumnious accusation against the friends of the slave.

The Abolitionists might, perhaps, make decisions in the case not wide of the mark, founded upon the rule given by Jesus Christ: "By their fruits ye shall know them." But, in declaring that slaveholders ought not to be fellowshipped as Christians, they do not say whether a slaveholder is or is not a Christian. On the contrary, they leave each one with his Maker, the INFALLIBLE JUDGE. But this they do:—they hold that no slaveholder, professing to be a Christian, is entitled to Christian FELLOWSHIP, *because* slaveholding is a sin, and should subject the offender to discipline. Neither Dr. Chalmers nor any other divine could deny the propriety of this, provided they believed that slaveholding is a sin, or an ecclesiastical offence. The apostle Paul directed that Christians should not *eat* with an *extortioner*. A slaveholder is an extortioner. If, then, a Christian may not eat a common meal with such an offender, may he sit at the Lord's table with him? I trow not.

LEWIS TAPPAN.

A Leaf from my Scrap Book.

MAY, 1849.

SAMUEL R. WARD AND FREDERICK DOUGLASS.

PERHAPS a fitter occasion never presented itself, nor was more properly availed of, for the exhibition of talent, than when Frederick Douglass and Samuel R. Ward debated the "question" whether the Constitution was or not a pro-slavery document.

With the "question" at issue we have, at present, nothing to do; and with the arguments so far only as they exhibit the men.

Both eminent for talent of an order (though differing somewhat in cast) far above the common level of great men.

If any inequalities existed, they served rather to heighten than diminish the interest of the occasion, giving rise to one of the severest contests of mind with mind that has yet come to my notice.

Douglass, sincere in the opinions he has espoused, defends them with a fervor and eloquence that finds scarcely a competitor.

In his very look—his gesture—in his whole manner, there is so much of genuine, earnest eloquence, that they leave no time for reflection. Now you are reminded of one rushing down some fearful steep, bidding you follow; now on some delightful stream, still beckoning you onward.

In either case, no matter what your prepossessions or oppositions, you for the moment, at least, forget the justness or unjustness of his cause and obey the summons, and loath, if at all, you return to your former post.

Not always, however, is he successful in retaining you. Giddy as you may be with the descent you have made, delighted as you are with the pleasure afforded, with the elysium to which he has wafted you, you return too often dissatisfied with his and your own impetuosity and want of firmness. You feel that you had had only a dream, a pastime, not a reality.

This great power of momentary captivation consists in his eloquence of manner—his just appreciation of words.

In listening to him, your whole soul is fired—every nerve strung—every passion inflated—every faculty you possess ready to perform at a moment's bidding. You stop not to ask why or wherefore.

'Tis a unison of mighty yet harmonious sounds that play upon your imagination; and you give yourself up, for a time, to their irresistible charm.

At last, the *cataract* which roared around you is hushed, the *tornado* is passed, and you find yourself sitting upon a bank (at whose base roll but tranquil waters), quietly meditating that why, amid such a display of power, no greater effect had really been produced.

After all, it must be admitted, there is a power in Mr. Douglass rarely to be found in any other man.

With copiousness of language, and finish of diction, when even ideas fail, words come to his aid—arranging themselves, as it were, so completely, that they not only captivate, but often deceive us for ideas; and hence the vacuum that would necessarily occur in the address of an ordinary *speaker* is filled up, presenting the same beautiful harmony as do the lights and shades of a picture.

From Mr. Douglass, in this, perhaps, as much as in any other respect, does Mr. *Ward* differ. Ideas form the basis of all Mr. Ward utters. Words are only used to express those ideas.

If words and ideas are not inseparable, then, as mortar is to the stones that compose the building, so are his words to his ideas.

In this, I judge, lays Mr. Ward's greatest strength. Concise without abruptness—without extraordinary stress, always clear and forcible; if sparing of ornament, never inelegant. In all, there appears a consciousness of strength, developed by close study and deep reflection, and only put forth because the occasion demanded,—a power not only to examine but to enable you to see the fairness of that examination and the justness of its conclusions.

You feel Douglass to be right, without always seeing it; perhaps it is not too much to say, when Ward is right you see it.

His appeals are directed rather to the understanding than the imagination; but so forcibly do they take possession of it, that the heart unhesitatingly yields.

If, as we have said, Mr. Douglass seems as one

whirling down some steep descent whose very impetuosity impels;—ere you are aware of it, it is the quiet serenity of Mr. Ward, as he points up the rugged ascent, and invites you to follow, that inspires your confidence and ensures your safety. Step by step do you with him climb the rugged steep; and, as you gain each succeeding eminence, he points you to new scenes and new delights;—now grand—sublime; now picturesque and beautiful;—always real. Most speakers fail to draw a perfect figure. This point I think Mr. Ward has gained. His figures, when done, stand out with prominence, possessing both strength and elegance.

Douglass' imagery is fine—vivid—often gaudily painted. Ward's pictures—bold, strong, glowing.

Douglass speaks right on; you acknowledge him to have been on the ground—nay, to have gone over the field; *Ward* seeks for and finds the corners; sticks the stakes, and leaves them standing; we know where to find them.

Mr. Douglass deals in generals; Mr. Ward reduces everything to a point.

Douglass is the *lecturer;* Ward the *debater.* Douglass powerful in invective; Ward in argument. What advantage Douglass gains in mimicry Ward recovers in wit.

Douglass has sarcasm, Ward point.

Here, again, an essential difference may be pointed out:—

Douglass says much, at times, you regret he uttered. This, however, is the real man, and on reflection you like him the better for it. What Ward says you feel to be but a necessity, growing out of the case,—that it ought to have been said—that you would have said precisely the same yourself, without adding or diminishing a single sentence.

Douglass, in manner, is at all times pleasing; Ward seldom less so; often raises to the truly majestic, and never descends below propriety. If you regret when Douglass ceases to speak, you are anxious Ward should continue.

Dignity is an essential quality in an orator—I mean true dignity.

Douglass has this in an eminent degree; Ward no less so, coupled with it great self-possession. He is never disconcerted—all he desires he says.

In one of his replies to Mr. Douglass I was struck with admiration, and even delight, at the calm, dignified manner in which he expressed himself, and his ultimate triumph under what seemed to me very peculiar circumstances.

Douglass' was a splendid effort—a beautiful effusion. One of those outpourings from the deeps of his heart of which he can so admirably give existence to.

He had brought down thunders of well-merited applause; and sure I am, that a whisper, a breath from almost any other opponent than Mr. Ward, would have produced a tumult of hisses.

Not so, however, now. The quiet, majestic air, the suppressed richness of a deep-toned, but well-cultivated voice, as the speaker paid a few well-timed compliments to his opponents, disturbed not, as it had produced, the dead stillness around.

Next followed some fine sallies of wit, which broke in on the calm.

He then proceeded to make and accomplished one of the most finished speeches to which I have ever listened, and sat down amidst a perfect storm of cheers.

It was a noble burst of eloquence,—the gatherings up of the choicest possible culled thoughts, and poured forth, mingling with a unison of brilliant flashes and masterly strokes, following each other in quick succession; and though felt—deeply felt, no more to be described than the vivid lightning's zig-zag, as produced from the deep-charged thunder-cloud.

If Douglass is not always successful in his attempts to heave up his ponderous missiles at his opponents, from the point of his descent, he always shows determination and spirit.

He is often too far down the *pass*, however, (herculean though he be,) for his intent.

Ward, from the eminence he has gained, giant-like, hurls them back with the force and skill of a practised marksman, almost invariably to the detriment of his already fallen victim.

In Douglass you have a man, in whose soul the iron of oppression has far entered, and you feel it.

He tells the story of his wrongs, so that they stand out in all their naked ugliness.

In Ward, you have one with strong native powers, —I know of none stronger; superadded a careful and extensive cultivation; an understanding so matured, that fully enables him to successfully grapple with men or errors, and portray truth in a manner equalled by few.

After all, it must be admitted, both are men of extraordinary powers of mind.

Both well qualified for the task they have undertaken.

I have, rather than anything else, drawn these outline portraits for our *young men*, who can fill them up at leisure.

The subjects are both fine models, and may be studied with profit by all,—especially those who are destined to stand in the front rank.

William J. Wilson

NOTE.—It has been some years since the above sketch was drawn; and though my impressions, especially of Mr. Douglass, has undergone some slight change since,—seeing in him enlarged, strengthened, and more matured thought, still I think, on the whole, the careful observer will attest substantially to its correctness.

"Who is my Neighbor?"

IT gives me great pleasure to express my interest in your objects, by the following sentiment: Sympathy for the slave,—the clearest exhibition in modern times of the spirit which, in the parable of the Samaritan, first illumined the wrong of oppression, and the divineness of brotherly love.

Th. Starr King

Consolation for the Slave.

SLAVE though thou art to unfeeling power,
Till wrong shall reach her final hour,
Mourn not as one on whom the day
Will never shed a healing ray.
The star of hope, that leads the dawn,
Appears, and night will soon be gone.

Long has thy night of sorrow been,
Without a star to cheer the scene.
Nay; there was One that watched and wept,
When thou didst think all mercy slept;
That eye, which beams with love divine,
Where all celestial glories shine.

Justice will soon the sceptre take;
The scourge shall fall, the tyrant quake.

Hark! 'tis the voice of One from heaven;
The word, the high command is given,
"Break every yoke, loose every chain,
To usher in the Saviour's reign."

Samuel Willard

The Key.

THE Key to Uncle Tom's Cabin: a key to unlock any mind that is not rendered inaccessible by the rust of conservatism or party-spirit, and to open the fountain of every generous affection, which is not closed with impenetrable ice. With this key may every one become familiar, who would know, and both in word and deed "bear witness to the truth!"

Samuel Willard

The True Mission of Liberty.

IF Liberty were to go on a pilgrimage all over the earth, she would find a home in every house, and a welcome in every heart. None would reject the favors she offers if brought to their own doors. Sure and prompt as the impulses of instinct, every bosom would open to admit her and her blessings, but—when her gospel is proclaimed as a common bounty to all the world,—when she is seen visiting and feasting with publicans and sinners, and sitting with her unwashed disciples in familiar and loving companionship, Cæsar and the synagogue are alike alarmed and enraged. When she is found daily in the market-place and on the mountain-top, in the hamlet and on the highway, ministering to the multitude, healing and feeding them,—showing the same love and reverence for humanity in every variety of conditions, and however disguised or degraded,—the cruelty of caste and the bitterness of bigotry straightway take counsel among themselves how they may destroy her.

Heaven help us! Divided as we are, into the hating and the hated, the oppressors and the oppressed, we have settled it, somehow, that we are of necessity at war with each other—that the welfare of one in some way depends upon the wretchedness of another. How much madness and misery would be spared if we could in any way learn that we are brethren.

William Elliot

The true Spirit of Reform.

THE religion of Jesus, acting as a vital principle in the individual heart, and thus leaving the entire mass of humanity, to this alone are we to look as of sufficient power to do away the evils that are now rife in the world. Just so far as the true spirit of Jesus is infused into the soul, and acts in the life of man, we know that sin, in its various forms of sensuality, oppression, and bloodshed, must disappear. All reforms, which are not based on this corner-stone, are superficial; and, however goodly their proportions may appear to the eye of man, they want that firm foundation which will secure them against being undermined or overthrown by the force of adverse circumstances. "Other foundation can no man lay, than that is laid," for the building up of all that is really excellent and heavenly.

But, while we acknowledge the omnipotence of true religion for the ratification of all social wrongs, we are not to rest in the inculcation of its abstract principles and outward forms alone. It is not enough that we ourselves become, or persuade our fellow-men to become professed disciples of Jesus; not enough that, in a general way, we urge the precepts of the gospel. The obtuseness of the human heart, when hardened by habit and early education, requires that we make particular application of the precepts of Christ, and address our efforts to the removal of specific sins: the sins of our own age and country. It may be that our brother, sincerely intending to act in the spirit of Jesus, is yet blinded by the force of habit, and fails to see the sin in which he is living. If our position make us to see more clearly than he the course he should pursue, let us endeavor gently to remove the veil from his eyes, remembering how often our own vision is dimmed by prejudice and outward circumstances. In the moral, as well as in the natural world, we believe that God demands our active coöperation; and, as the farmer not only sows the seed, but roots out the weeds from among the grain, so are we to endeavor to eradicate from the broad field of the moral world those evil practices which obstruct the growth of the harvest of pure and undefiled religion.

"The husbandman waiteth for the precious fruit of the earth, and hath long patience for it, until he receive the early and latter rain." So are we obliged often to have "long patience," until we see the manifest blessing of God on our labors. But patient waiting becomes a virtue, only when combined with the exercise of our best powers in promoting the object of our desire. We must adapt our efforts to the express object which we seek to attain. Taking those spiritual weapons which are "mighty for the pulling down of the strongholds" of sin, let us assault the great evils of slavery and oppression of every name and kind, always marching under the banners of the Prince of Peace, whose conquests are achieved not by violence, but by the subduing power of Godlike love. Let us go forth, brethren, sisters, a feeble band though we may seem to the eye of man, yet strong in the assurance that the hosts of heaven are encamped round about us, and that "more are they that are with us, than they that are" on the side of the oppressor; and let us not falter until in God's own good time the word shall be spoken, not as, we would hope, in the whirlwind or the earthquake, but in the "still small voice" of the oppressor's own conviction, saying to the slaves, "Go free!"

Mary W. Willard

A Welcome to Mrs. H. B. Stowe, on her Return from Europe.

SHE comes, she comes, o'er the bounding wave,
Borne swift as an eagle's flight;
She comes, the tried friend of the slave,—
Truth's champion for the right.

Not as the blood-stained warrior comes,
With shrill-sounding fife and drums;
But peaceful by our quiet homes,
The conquering heroine comes.

Then welcome to our Pilgrim shore,
Tho' sad affliction* meet thee;
Three million welcomes from God's poor,
The south winds bear, to greet thee.

* The sickness of her daughter.

To thee, with chain-linked hearts we come,
Which naught but death can sever,
To thank thee for thy "Uncle Tom,"
Thy gentle-hearted "Eva."

When the crushed slave himself shall own,
Three million fetters broken,
Shall mount before thee, to the Throne;
Of thy true life, the token.

Then welcome to our northern hills;
Thy own New England dwelling;
The birds, the trees, the sparkling rills,
All, are thy welcome swelling.

Joseph C. Holly.

ROCHESTER, N. Y., October 19th, 1853.

Forward.

FROM THE GERMAN OF HOFFMAN, IN FOLLERSLEBEN.

It is a time of swell and flood,
We linger on the strand,
And all that might to us bring good
Lies in the distant land.

O forward! forward! why stand still?
The flood will ne'er run dry;
Who through the wave not venture will,
That land shall never spy.

T. W. Higginson.

What has Canada to do with Slavery?

THE question is often asked, both in Canada and in the United States: What have we in Canada to do with the Institution of Slavery, as it exists in the neighboring Republic? I do not think that a better answer is necessary, than that which is contained in the following extracts—the former of which is taken from a speech delivered by George Thompson, Esq., at the formation of the Anti-Slavery Society of Canada—the latter from the valuable work of the Rev. Albert Barnes on Slavery:

"Are we separated geographically and politically from the country where slavery reigns? We are, for that very reason, the persons best able to form an unbiassed and sound judgment on the question at issue. We have as much to do with this question as with any question that concerns the happiness of man, the glory of God, or the hopes and destinies of the human race. We have to do with this question, for it lies at the foundation of our own rights as a portion of the human family. The cause of liberty is one all over the world. What have you to do with this question? The slave is your brother, and you cannot dissolve that Union. While he remains God's child he will remain your brother. He is helpless, and you are free and powerful; and if you neglect him, you are not doing as you would have others do to you, were you in bonds. Know you not that it is God's method to save man by man, and that man is only great, and honorable, and blest himself, as he is the friend and defender of those who need his aid. You are dwellers on the same continent with three millions of slaves. Their sighs come to you with every breeze from the South. Oh, haste to help them, that this glorious continent may be freed from its pollution and its curse."

Extract from Barnes on slavery:

"Slavery pertains to a great wrong done to our common nature, and affects great questions, relating to the final triumph of the principles of justice and humanity. The race is one great brotherhood, and every man is under obligation, as far as he has the ability, to defend those principles which will permanently promote the welfare of the human family. * * * * The questions of right and wrong know no geographical limits; are bounded by no conventional lines; are circumscribed by the windings of no river or stream, and are not designated by climate or by the course of the sun. There are no enclosures within which the question of right and wrong may not be carried with the utmost freedom."

Other answers might be given, but these are quite sufficient.

Thomas Henning

The Fugitive Slave Bill: a Fragment.

BUT ours is the saddest part of this sad business. It would be hard enough to live surrounded by bondmen, even though we had never known any other way of life. Still, for one who had grown up with young slaves for playmates and for nurses, there might be much in the relation to quiet the conscience and soothe the sensibilities. Strong attachments, we all know, are often realized, even in a condition of things so anomalous. Perhaps, too, a large number of those about us would be as feeble in capacity as humble in their circumstances. One so born might tolerate such a position. But how different,—how, in comparison, and in every way intolerable, to be set as watchmen and interceptors of these, the brighter and the better, who, beyond all controversy, have outgrown the estate of bondage, and who are so loudly called of God to be freemen, that they will brave any peril in obedience to the call! How can we do this and still be men and Christians? Would our brethren at the south do it for us? If we have, in our haste, so covenanted, must we not rather pay the penalty than fulfil the bond? I recognize obedience to civil government as the solemn duty of all save *those who without cause are made outlaws by the State.* Government protects our hearths and shelters those who are dearest to us. But we can honor the law by submitting to its penalties as well as by complying with its demands, and the penalty would be my election when a man who had seized his manhood at the peril of his life should claim of me shelter and the means of escape. Before I refuse that, "may my right hand forget its cunning and my tongue cleave to the roof of my mouth."

Rufus Ellis.

The Encroachment of the Slave-Power.

EXTRACT.

SUCH is the unholy and gigantic power that, leaving its territorial domain, has usurped the seat of freedom—that has established at our capitol a central despotism, and bends to its will with iron hand the Legislative, Executive, and Judicial branches of our Federal Government.

I have marvelled, sir, as you have, that the Spirit of Freedom in our fair land has so long slumbered beneath such an outrage, But I imagine her awakening. As she is about to awaken in her strength, and with the voice of the people, like the sound of many waters, rebuking this insolent slave-power, as Milton tells us its father and inventor was of old rebuked, as he sought to pass the bounds of his prison-house, and to darken with his presence the realms of light—

"And reckon'st thou thyself with spirits of Heaven,
Hell-doom'd! and breath'st defiance here and scorn,
Where I reign King, and to enrage thee more
Thy King and Lord? Back to thy punishment
False fugitive, and to thy speed add wings,
Lest with a whip of scorpions I pursue
Thy lingering, or with one stroke of this dart,
Strange horrors seize thee and pangs unfelt before."

Faithfully yours,

John Jay

The Dishonor of Labor.

THE fundamental, essential cause of slavery and its concomitants, ignorance, degradation and suffering on the one side, as of idleness, prodigality and luxury-born disease on the other, is a false idea of the nature and offices of Labor.

Labor is not truly a curse, as has too long been asserted. It only becomes such through human perverseness, misconception and sin. It was no curse to the first pair in Eden, and will not be to their descendants, whenever and wherever the spirit of Eden shall pervade them. It is only a curse because too many seek to engross the product of others' work, yet do little or none themselves. If the secret were but out, *that no man can really enjoy more than his own moderate daily labor would produce*, and *none can truly enjoy this without doing the work*, the death-knell of Slavery in

Horace Greeley.

general—in its subtler as well as its grosser forms—would be rung. Until that truth shall be thoroughly diffused, the cunning and strong will be able to prey upon the simple and feeble, whether the latter be called slaves or something else.

The great reform required is not a work of hours nor of days, but of many years. It must first pervade our literature, and thence our current ideas and conversation, before it can be infused into the common life. Meanwhile, it would be well to remember that—

Every man who exchanges business for idleness, not because he has become too old or infirm to work, but because he has become rich enough to live without work;

Every man who educates his son for a profession, rather than a mechanical or agricultural calling, not because of that son's supposed fitness for the former rather than the latter, but because he imagines Law, Physic or Preaching, a more respectable, genteel vocation, than building houses or growing grain;

Every maiden who prefers in marriage a rich suitor of doubtful morals or scanty brains to a poor one, of sound principles, blameless life, good information and sound sense;

Every mother who is pleased when her daughter receives marked attention from a rich lawyer or merchant, but frowns on the addresses of a young farmer or artisan of slender property, but of well-stored mind, good character and industrious, provident habits;

Every young man who, in choosing the sharer of his fireside and the future mother of his children, is less solicitous as to what she is good for, than as to how much she is worth;

Every youth who is trained to regard little work and much recompense—short business-hours and long dinners—as the chief ends of exertion and as assurances of a happy life;

Every teacher who thinks more of the wages than of the opportunities for usefulness afforded by his or her vocation;

Every rich Abolitionist, who is ashamed of being caught by distinguished visiters while digging in his garden or plowing in the field, and wishes them to understand that he so works, not for occupation, but for pastime; and

Every Abolition lecturer who would send a hireling two miles after a horse, whereon to ride three miles to fulfil his next appointment respectably;

Though meaning no such thing, and perhaps shocked when it is suggested, is a practical and powerful upholder of the continued enslavement of our fellow-men.

In the faith of the "good time coming,"

I remain yours,

HORACE GREELEY.

NEW YORK, NOV. 7, 1853.

The Evils of Colonization

I SPEAK the words of soberness and truth when I say, that the most inveterate, the most formidable, the deadliest enemy of the peace, prosperity, and happiness of the colored population of the United States, is that system of African colonization which originated in and is perpetuated by a worldly, Pharoah-like policy beneath the dignity of a magnanimous and Christian people;—a system which receives much of its vitality from *ad captandum* appeals to popular prejudices, and to the unholy, grovelling passions of the canaille;—a system that interposes every possible obstacle in the way of the improvement and elevation of the colored man in the land of his birth;—that instigates the enactment of laws whose design and tendency are obviously to annoy him, to make him feel, while at home, that he is a stranger and a pilgrim—nay more,—to make him "wretched, and miserable, and poor, and blind, and naked;"—to make him "a hissing and a by-word," "a fugitive and a vagabond" throughout the American Union;—a system that is so irreconcilably opposed to the purpose of God in making "of *one* blood all nations for to dwell on *all* the face of the earth," that when the dying slaveholder, under the lashes of a guilty conscience, would give to his slaves unqualified freedom, it wickedly interposes, and persuades him that "to do justly and love mercy" would be to inflict an irreparable injury upon the community, and that to do his duty to God and his fellow-creatures, under the circumstances, he should bequeath to his surviving slaves the cruel alternative of *either expatriation to a far-off, pestilential clime, with the prospect of a premature death, or perpetual slavery, with its untold horrors, in his native land.* Against this most iniquitous system of persecution and proscription of an inoffensive people, for no other reason than that we wear the physical exterior given us in infinite wisdom and benevolence, I would record, nay *engrave* with the pen of a diamond, my most emphatic and solemn protest; more especially would I do so, as the system, under animadversion, is most inconsistently fostered, and shamelessly lauded, by ministers of the gospel in the nineteenth century, as a scheme of Christian philanthropy! "O my soul, come not thou into their secret; unto their assembly, mine honor, be not thou united."

Wm J Watkins

TORONTO, C. W., Oct. 31st.

William H Seward.

The Basis of the American Constitution

"HAPPY," (said Washington, when announcing the treaty of peace to the army,) "thrice happy shall they be pronounced hereafter, who shall have contributed anything, who shall have performed the meanest office in erecting this stupendous fabric of freedom and empire on the broad basis of independency, who shall have assisted in protecting the Rights of Human Nature, and establishing an asylum for the poor and oppressed of all nations and religions."

You remember well that the Revolutionary Congress in the declaration of independence placed the momentous controversy between the Colonies and Great Britain on the absolute and inherent equality of all men. It is not, however, so well understood that that body closed its existence on the adoption of the Federal Constitution with this solemn injunction, addressed to the people of the United States: "Let it be remembered that it has ever been the pride and boast of America, that the Rights for which she contended were the Rights of Human Nature."

No one will contend that our Fathers, after effecting the Revolution and the independence of their country, by proclaiming this system of beneficent political philosophy, established an entirely different one in the constitution assigned to its government. This philosophy, then, is the basis of the American Constitution.

It is, moreover, a true philosophy, deduced from the nature of man and the character of the Creator. If there were no supreme law, then the world would be a scene of universal anarchy, resulting from the eternal conflict of peculiar institutions and antagonistic laws. There being such a universal law, if any human constitution and laws differing from it could have any authority, then that universal law could not be supreme. That supreme law is necessarily based on the equality of nations, of races, and of men. It is a simple, self-evident basis. One nation, race, or individual, may not oppress or injure another, because the safety and welfare of each is essential to the common safety and welfare of all. If all are not equal and free, then who is entitled to be free, and what evidence of his superiority can he bring from nature or revelation? All men necessarily have a common interest in the promulgation and maintenance of these principles, because it is equally in the nature of men to be content with the enjoyment of their just rights, and to be discontented under the privation of them. Just so far as these principles practically prevail, the stringency of government is safely relaxed, and peace and harmony obtain. But men cannot maintain these principles, or even comprehend them, without a very considerable advance in knowledge and virtue. The law of nations, designed to preserve peace among mankind, was unknown to the ancients. It has been perfected in our own times, by means of the more general dissemination of knowledge and practice of the virtues inculcated by Christianity. To disseminate knowledge, and to increase virtue therefore among men, is to establish and maintain the principles on which the recovery and preservation of their inherent natural rights depend; and the State that does this most faithfully, advances most effectually the common cause of Human Nature.

For myself, I am sure that this cause is not a

dream, but a reality. Have not all men consciousness of a property in the memory of human transactions available for the same great purposes, the security of their individual rights, and the perfection of their individual happiness? Have not all men a consciousness of the same equal interest in the achievements of invention, in the instructions of philosophy, and in the solaces of music and the arts? And do not these achievements, instructions, and solaces, exert everywhere the same influences, and produce the same emotions in the bosoms of all men? Since all languages are convertible into each other, by correspondence with the same agents, objects, actions, and emotions, have not all men practically one common language? Since the constitutions and laws of all societies are only so many various definitions of the rights and duties of men as those rights and duties are learned from Nature and Revelation, have not all men practically one code of moral duty? Since the religions of men, in their various climes, are only so many different forms of their devotion towards a Supreme and Almighty Power entitled to their reverence and receiving it under the various names of Jehovah, Jove, and Lord, have not all men practically one religion?

Since all men are seeking liberty and happiness for a season here, and to deserve and so to secure more perfect liberty and happiness somewhere in a future world, and, since they all substantially agree that these temporal and spiritual objects are to be attained only through the knowledge of truth and the practice of virtue, have not mankind practically one common pursuit through one common way of one common and equal hope and destiny?

If there had been no such common Humanity as I have insisted upon, then the American people would not have enjoyed the sympathies of mankind when establishing institutions of civil and religious liberty here, nor would their establishment here have awakened in the nations of Europe and of South America desires and hopes of similar institutions there. If there had been no such common Humanity, then we should not ever, since the American Revolution, have seen human society throughout the world divided into two parties, the high and the low—the one perpetually foreboding and earnestly hoping the downfall, and the other as confidently predicting and as sincerely desiring, the durability of Republican Institutions. If there had been no such common

Humanity, then we should not have seen this tide of emigration from insular and continental Europe flowing into our country through the channels of the St. Lawrence, the Hudson, and the Mississippi,—ebbing, however, always with the occasional rise of the hopes of freedom abroad, and always swelling again into greater volume when those premature hopes subside. If there were no such common Humanity, then the poor of Great Britain would not be perpetually appealing to us against the oppression of landlords on their farms and work-masters in their manufactories and mines; and so, on the other hand, we should not be, as we are now, perpetually framing apologies to mankind for the continuance of African slavery among ourselves. If there were no such common Humanity, then the fame of Wallace would have long ago died away in his native mountains, and the name even of Washington would at most have been only a household word in Virginia, and not as it is now, a watchword of Hope and Progress throughout the world.

If there had been no such common Humanity, then when the civilization of Greece and Rome had been consumed by the fires of human passion, the nations of modern Europe could never have gathered from among its ashes the philosophy, the arts, and the religion, which were imperishable, and have reconstructed with those materials that better civilization, which, amid the conflicts and fall of political and ecclesiastical systems, has been constantly advancing towards perfection in every succeeding age. If there had been no such common Humanity, then the dark and massive Egyptian obelisk would not have everywhere reappeared in the sepulchral architecture of our own times, and the light and graceful orders of Greece and Italy would not as now have been the models of our villas and our dwellings, nor would the simple and lofty arch and the delicate tracery of Gothic design have been as it now is, everywhere consecrated to the service of religion.

If there had been no such common humanity, then would the sense of the obligation of the Decalogue have been confined to the despised nation who received it from Mount Sinai, and the prophecies of Jewish seers and the songs of Jewish bards would have perished forever with their temple, and never afterwards could they have become as they now are, the universal utterance of the spiritual emotions and hopes of mankind. If there had been no such common humanity, then certainly Europe and Africa, and even new America, would not, after the lapse of centuries, have recognized a common Redeemer, from all the sufferings and perils of human life, in a culprit who had been ignominiously executed in the obscure Roman province of Judea; nor would Europe have ever gone up in arms to Palestine, to wrest from the unbelieving Turk the tomb where that culprit had slept for only three days and nights after his descent from the cross,—much less would his traditionary instructions, preserved by fishermen and publicans, have become the chief agency in the renovation of human society, through after-coming ages.

WM. H. SEWARD.

A Wish

"Could I embody and unbosom now,
That which is most within me;—could I wreak
My thoughts upon expression, and thus throw
Soul, heart, mind, passions, feelings strong or weak,
All that I would have sought, and all I seek,
Bear, know, and feel, and breathe,—into *one* word,
And that one word were lightning."—

I would speak it, not to crush the oppressor, but to melt the chains of slave and master, so that *both* should go free.

Caroline M. Kirkland.

New York, November 8th, 1853.

A Dialogue.

SCENE.—A BREAKFAST TABLE.

MRS. GOODMAN, *a widow.*
FRANK GOODMAN, *her son.*
MR. FREEMAN, *a Southern gentleman, brother to Mrs. Goodman.*
MR. DRYMAN, *a boarder.*

MR. FREEMAN. (*Sipping his coffee and looking over the morning paper*) reads—

"The performance of Uncle Tom's Cabin attracts to the theatre very unusual audiences. In the "genteel row" last evening, we observed the strictest religionists of the day, not excepting puritanic Presbyterians, and the sober disciples of Wesley and Fox. For ourselves, we must candidly confess we have never witnessed such a *play* upon all the emotions of which humanity is susceptible. Mrs. Stowe, however unworthy the name of Patriot, is at least entitled to the credit of seizing the great thought of the age, and embodying it in such a form as to make it presentable to every order of mind and every class of society. She says, in effect, to Legislators, let me furnish your amusements, and I care not who makes your laws."

Politicians would do well to look to this—(*laying down the paper and speaking in a tone of impatience*)—so, so, Fanaticism is leading to its legitimate results. Uncle Tom in our parlors, Uncle Tom in our pulpits, and Uncle Tom in our plays.

Mr. Dryman. Truly "he eateth with publicans and sinners."

Mr. F. (*Not noticing Mr. D.'s remark.*) One would think this last appropriation of the vaunted hero would be sufficient to convince the most radical of the demoralizing influence of these publications.

Frank. (*Modestly.*) How differently people judge. Why, last evening, when I saw crowds of the hardened and dissipated shedding tears of honest sympathy, when Uncle Tom and Eva sang,

> "I see a band of spirits bright,
> And conquering palms they bear"—

I felt that the moral sentiment was asserting its supremacy even in places of amusement.

Mr. F. Worse and worse, my nephew and namesake a theatre-goer.

Mr. D. (*In an under tone.*) Namesake! "that's the unkindest cut of all."

Frank. Not exactly a theatre-goer, uncle, though I confess I might be, were the performance always as excellent as last evening.

Mrs. Goodman. Frank, my son, I hope thee will not attempt to drink from a dirty pool because a pure stream flows into it.

Frank. But the rank and file of Democracy drank deep libations to Liberty there, mother.

Mr. D. (*Passing his cup.*) "Drink deep or taste not of the Pierian spring."

Mr. F. (*Sarcastically.*) Take care, you'll be found using the products of slave labor!

Frank. (*Jocosely.*)

> "Think how many backs have smarted,
> For the sweets," &c.

Take a bit of toast, Mr. Dryman, our northern products are perfectly innocent, you know?

Mr. D. (*Helping himself bountifully.*) "Ask no questions for conscience's sake."

Mr. F. The practice of you Northerners is consistent with your professions.

Mr. D. "Consistency, thou art a jewel!"

Frank. It is very hard to be consistent in this world, uncle. My mother once made a resolution to use nothing polluted by Intemperance or Oppression, but finding that it required her to take constant thought "what we should eat and drink, and wherewithal we should be clothed," she was fain to relax her discipline.

Mrs. G. Frank, thee must not transcend the truth in thy mirthfulness.

Frank. Well, mother, did not some experiment of the kind lead to the conclusion, that I might exercise my freedom in worldly amusements?

Mrs. G. Yes, my son, but thy enthusiasm about the theatre makes me fear I have gone beyond my light.

Mr. F. (*Bitterly.*) Never fear, sister, the young man will soon prove that Abolition Societies and Theatres are admirable schools of morals.

Frank. Uncle Tom at least has a good moral, and so has William Tell and Pizarro—indeed I do not remember of ever reading a play which had not.

Mr. F. (*In a tone of irony.*) When I see a young

man spending his time at the theatre, in search of good morals, I think he "pays too dear for his whistle."

Mrs. G. And yet brother Frank speaks the truth. What success does thee think a play would meet, which should represent such a man as Uncle Tom yielding his principles and faith to the will of a Legree?"

Mr. F. (*With great asperity.*) Do you, too, Rebecca, advocate theatres?

Mrs. G. It is not of theatres, but of books, that I am speaking. Does thee recollect any work, the whole plot and design of which is made to turn upon the triumph of the wicked over the good?

Mr. F. (*Musing.*) Why—I—don't remember now—

Frank (*In great surprise.*) Why, mother, are there no books written in favor of Slavery?

Mrs. G. I cannot think of any book which can be said to be written for Slavery, in the sense that Uncle Tom's Cabin is written against it. Such a work is, I think, impossible. No poet would attempt to portray its moral aspects, and delineate its beauties, with the idea of exciting our admiration and approval.

Mr. F. Spoken just like a woman! Your sex always seize upon some thought gained through the sensibilities, and then bring in a decision without farther investigation.

Frank. And is not the instinct of a woman a more perfect guide in morals, than the reason of man?

Mr. F. (*Sarcastically.*) Certainly—if it direct her son to the theatre.

Mr. D. Or teach him the supremacy of the "Higher Law."

Frank. (*With warmth.*) My mother did not direct me to the theatre, sir; she has taught me to love better things;—to her I owe all the lofty sentiments of virtue and truth.

Mrs. G. Softly, softly Frank, theatres and Slavery will be quite sufficient for this discussion, without introducing Woman's Rights. (*To Mr. Freeman.*) Would it not be more consistent, brother, for thee to disprove my argument, than to object to my method of obtaining it?

Mr. F. Nothing can be easier—you have asserted in round terms that no work was ever written in favor of Slavery. What an absurdity! If you have any information you must know that the southern press groans with publications upon this topic.

Mrs. G. Still if thee examine the matter, thee will

find that every one of these books treats Slavery as a curse, and describes it not as a *good* but an *evil*, of which each man loads the guilt upon his forefathers or his neighbors.

Mr. F. Granted they call it a curse, but assuredly they bring forward a defence.

Mrs. G. Yes, they defend the Constitution; they defend the rights of the south; they advocate Colonization, or point out the errors of Abolitionists, but what one in word or in effect advocates the principles of human Slavery? The truth is, brother, the system has the literature of the world against it; and the south ought to see in this reading age an infallible sign that the days of its cherished institutions are numbered. Does thee not perceive that every novel and every poem carries to the parlor, or, if it please thee, to the theatre, an influence which will eventually re-act on the ballot-box.

Frank. Do you mean, mother, to include in your remarks the discourses of Reverend Divines upon the Patriarchal Institution?

Mrs. G. I cannot except even these; for they acknowledge it an evil, though they contend its exists by divine ordination, just as they assert Original Sin to be the offspring of Eternal Decrees; but they no more convince the Slaveholder, that he loves his bondman as himself, than they convict him of the guilt of Adam's transgression.

Mr. F. What do you say to Webster's great speech on the compromise measure?

Mrs. G. (*Pleasantly.*) Is not the moral view of a question, about as far as a woman's instinct ought to go?

Mr. F. Oh, no; go on, your strictures are quite amusing.

Mrs. G. Well, then, since *we* have taken the position of a reviewer, *we* must confess that the last effort of the great Daniel appears to us to be *on an Act of Congress.*

Mr. D. And *at* the Presidential chair.

Mrs. G. (*Continuing.*) It did not touch the merits of slavery at all. Webster knew the feelings of the constituents too well to attempt such a task. He therefore skilfully diverted their attention from his real issue, to the glorious Union, and its danger from agitators, and he thus carried with him the sympathies of many honest haters of oppression.

Mr. F. Well, sister, I do not know but you will

prove that there is not an advocate for slavery on the face of the earth.

Mrs. G. Only such advocates as there is for robbery and war. Those who find it for their interest to practice these crimes condemn them in the abstract, or at most only apologize for them, as necessary and expedient, under peculiar circumstances.

Frank. (*Laughing.*) Why, mother, I shall certainly subscribe for your "North American Review," particularly if you fill the literary department as ably as you have the moral and political, to test which, let me propound a question? If the reward of the good be the charm of fiction, how do you account for the pleasure derived from tragedy, where the good are overwhelmed with the evil?

Mrs. G. (*Smiling.*) With great diffidence we reply to the query of our learned friend. The force of tragedy consists in its depicting evil so ruinous as to involve even the innocent in the catastrophe; the pleasure is derived, we think, from the *failure* of the mischievous design, and the merited retribution which falls upon the head of the plotters. In Romeo, "a scourge is laid upon the hate of the Montagues and Capulets, by which all are punished;" Hamlet's wicked uncle is justly served, drinking the poison tempered by himself; and Iago pulls down ruin upon himself no less than upon Cassio.

Frank. (*Bowing playfully.*) Your review meets my entire approbation, inasmuch as it confirms my doctrine, that theatres always give their verdict in favor of virtue.

Mr. D. "Casting out devils through Beelzebub."

Mrs. G. The artistic effect of every work of the imagination is wrought upon what critics call the "sympathetic emotion of virtue," and the decisions of this faculty, so far as we understand them, always correspond with what Christians believe concerning the "final restitution of all things."

Frank. The theatre, then, ought to promote good morals—why does it not?

Mr. D.

> "And many worthy men
> Maintained it might be turned to good account,
> And so perhaps it might, but never was."

Mrs. G. The "sympathetic emotion of virtue," not having an object, never rises to passion, and therefore never produces action. Philosophers tell us that a thought of virtue passing often through the mind, without being wrought out into a fact, weakens the moral sense; thus people may read the best of books, and witness the finest exhibitions of moral beauty, and constantly retrograde in virtue. The dissolute characters of players, who continually utter the loftiest sentiments, and practice the lowest vices, are accounted for on this principle; and we ought to judge the theatre as we do slavery, by its demoralizing effect upon those engaged in it.

Mr. F. Do you mean to say, Rebecca, that slaveholding has the same effect upon me that stage-playing has upon the actor?

Mrs. G. Well, brother, I put it to thy own conscience. Does thee not, daily, in dealing with thy slaves, stifle thy emotions of piety, generosity, and love, and is it not easier to do this now than it was twenty years ago, when, with a heart full of tenderness and truth, thee left us for thy southern home?

Mr. F. (*Rising and pacing the room with great agitation.*) Now, sister, you are going to introduce another absurdity! Do I practice the principles learned in the nursery? No, I do not! Do I believe "honesty is the best policy" and its kindred humbugs? Of course I don't! Show me the man who does? Do I follow the precepts of the sermon on the Mount? Not I! The man who should undertake to do so would make himself a perfect laughing-stock. I should like to see one of your northern hypocrites attempt it. Ha! ha! ha! "Lay not up treasure upon earth," and "take no thought for the morrow;" why, what else do people take thought for, either North or South? It is not what they shall eat, drink, or wear to-day, that worries them, but how they shall lay up something for themselves or their children hereafter. You silly women are always talking about righteousness, as if you really thought it could enter in human plans, but we men of the world, who have to wring the precious dollar from the hard hand of labor, know better! I tell you, Rebecca, I don't believe there is a business-man in your pious Quaker city even, who would dare acquaint his wife and daughters with all his little arrangements for amassing wealth. Ha! ha! ha! How the pretty things would stare at the tricks of the trade, and simper: "Is that right?" As though anybody thought business principles were gospel principles! As though they expected a man was going to love his neighbor as himself, when he was making a bargain with him! It provokes me to see you make yourself so ridiculous! You ought to know that every man *acts* on the principle, that "Wealth is the chief good;" and you ought to know, too, that there the slaveholders have the advantage of you entirely. They do right to work, and grind it out of the slaves on a large scale, and call Abraham and Moses to witness the patriarchal method, while your northern mercenaries scheme and speculate how they can turn a penny out of ignorance and poverty, and have not even the apology of a precedent for their meanness. Why, one of our generous southern planters is as far above one of your stingy shave-three-cents-on-a-yard-tradesmen, as Robin Hood is above a miserable tea-spoon burglar. The south sails under false colors, does it? What flag do your platform men give to the wind, I should like to know? What do they care for the Fugitive Slave Law? Half of them would help a runaway to Canada with as good a will as they'd eat their dinner. (*Coming close and sitting down, so as to look fixedly in her face.*) I'll tell you what, sister, the chivalry of the south responds to you northern Christians who prate so loud of brotherhood and charity, in the words of young Cancer to his mother—"*Libenter tuis præceptis obsequar, si te prius idem facientem videro.*"

Mrs. G. (*very gently.*) These strictures, brother, are too keenly just. They remind me of Kossuth's assertion, that there is not yet a Christian nation on the earth, nor yet a Christian church, that dare venture entirely upon the principles of the Gospel. Still, the aberration of reformers proves no more in favor of slavery, than the vices and miseries of civilized life prove that barbarism is the natural and happy state of the human race; nay, these very aberrations prove that a centripetal power counteracts the opposing force, and holds them within the genial influence of the sun of truth.

The law of spiritual gravitation is little understood. But thousands of philosophers are closely observing the phenomena, and carefully comparing them with the data given in the Sermon on the Mount; and it is not too much to hope that this generation will give to the world a Newton, whose moral mathematics shall demonstrate that the *law* of *love* is the true theory of individual and national prosperity.

Mr. F. Well, sister, I wish you much joy of your millennial state; but before the Sermon on the Mount becomes the code of nations, I guess you will find—

Mr. D. (*interrupting.*) "A little more grape, Captain Bragg!"

Frank. I tell you, uncle, "there's a good time coming." Mother is a prophet. I have watched her words all my life, and I never knew them fall to the ground.

Mrs. G. Observe, my friends, that the Sermon on the Mount puts blessing before requirement. If you accept these beatitudes as the gift of your Divine Master, you will find that obedience to the precepts which follow, is not the unwilling service of a bondsman, but the free and natural action of an unfranchised spirit.

C. A. Bloss

CLOVER STREET SEM., November 10th, 1853.

A Time of Justice will Come

WE are conscious of the odium that rests upon us. We feel that we are wronged; but we are not impatient for the righting of our wrongs. We bide our time. The men that shall come after us, will do us justice. The present generation of America cannot "judge righteous judgment," in the case of the uncompromising friends of freedom, religion, and law. They are so debauched and blinded by slavery, and by the perverse and low ideas of freedom, religion, and law, which it engenders, that they "call evil good, and good evil; put darkness for light, and light for darkness; put bitter for sweet, and sweet for bitter." They have been living out the lie of slavery so long, and have been, thereby, deadening their consciences so long, as to be now well nigh incapable of perceiving the wide and everlasting distinctions between truth and falsehood.

GERRITT SMITH.

Hope and Confidence.

O! WHAT a strange thing is the human heart!
With its youth, and its joy and fear!
It doats upon creatures that day-dreams impart,—
Full sorely it grieves when their beauties depart,
And weeps bitter tears over their bier.

The veriest gleamings that dart into birth,
Reveal to its being of light:
The dimliest shadows that flit upon earth,
Allure it, with promise of pleasure and mirth
In a country, where never is night.

It leaves the sure things of its own real home,
To pursue the mere phantoms of thought!
Well knowing, that certain, there soon must come,
An end to the visions, that so gladsome,
It bewilder'd, has eagerly sought.

Chas. L. Reason

It fleeth the wholesome prose of life,
With its riches all sure and told:
And scorning the beauties, that calmly in strife
Truth fashions, it longs for the things all rife
With glitter, and color, and gold.

It buildeth its home 'neath an ever calm sky,
Near streams wherein crown-jewels sleep,—
And there it reposeth: while soothingly nigh,
Some loved one, perchance, doth most wooingly sigh,
As the zephyrs all full-laden creep.

Thus it musingly wasteth its strength, in dreams
Of bliss, that can never prove true:
And ever it revels amid what seems,
A paradise smiling with Hope's warm beams,
And flowers all spangled with dew.

But, even as flowers are broken and fade,
And yield up their perfumes—their souls,—
So vanish the colors of which dreams are made,—
So perish the structures on which Hope is staid,
And the treasures to which the heart holds.

In vain docs it follow the wandering forms
  That promise, yet always recede :—
Too briefly the sunshine is darken'd by storms:
Hope minstrels it onward, yet never informs
  Of the dangers unseen, that impede.

The Heart trusts the outward: "Of man 'tis the whole."
  Thus Confidence clings to decay!
It feels the sweet homage that riches control,—
And laughs in contempt at the wealth of the soul:
  And behold! now, friends wait for their prey.

It trusteth in glory, and beauty, and youth,—
  In love-vows that ne'er are to die:
But soon the Death-king, in whose heart is no ruth,
Enfolds it,—and mounting aloft, of Truth
  Thus sings, as turns glassy the eye.

"There's nothing so lovely and bright below,
  As the shapes of the purified mind!
Nought surer to which the weak heart can grow,
On which it can rest, as it onward doth go,
  Than that Truth which its own tendrils bind.

"Yes! Truth opes within a pure sun-tide of bliss,
  And shows in its ever calm flood,
A transcript of regions, where no darkness is,
Where HOPE its conceptions may realize,
  And CONFIDENCE sleep in 'The Good.'"

Chas. L. Reason.

A Letter that Speaks for Itself.

To T—— M——.

DISINTERESTED benevolence, my dear sir, has nothing at all to do with abolitionism. Nay, I doubt very much if there is such a thing as disinterested benevolence; but be this as it may, there is no occasion for it in the anti-slavery ranks.

It is selfishness,—sheer selfishness, that has thus far carried on the war with slavery and wrong in all times; and selfishness must break the chains of the American slave.

Self-love has fixed the chain around the arm of every leader and every soldier in the American anti-slavery army. Where would William Lloyd Garrison have been to-day, if any combination of circumstances could have shut in his soul's deep hatred of oppression, and prevented its finding utterance in burning words?

He would have been dead and rotten. It is necessary to his own existence that he should work,—work for the slave; and in his work he gratifies all the strongest instincts of his nature, more completely than even the grossest sensualist can gratify *his*, by unlimited indulgence.

Gerritt Smith, too. Suppose he was compelled to hoard his princely fortune, or spend it as most others do! O dear! what a dyspeptic we should have in six months; and all the hydropathic institutes in the country could never keep him alive five years.

John P. Hale would soon be done with his rotund person and jovial face, if he could no longer send the sharp arrows of his wit and sarcasm into the consciences of his human-whipping neighbors.

It is a necessity of all great nations to hate meanness, and nothing under God's heaven ever was so mean as American slavery. Think of it. *Men* who swagger around with pistols and bowie-knifes to avenge their insulted honor, if any one should question it,—imagine one turning up his sleeves to horsewhip an old woman for burning his steak, or pocketing her wages, earned at the wash-tub!

No one with a soul above that of a pig-louse, could

help loathing the system, the instant he saw it in its native meanness. Then, in order to keep his own self-respect,—to gratify the love of the good and true in his own soul, he *must* express that loathing.

No disinterestedness about doing right, for nobody can be so much interested in the act as the doer of it.

Wrong-doing is the only possible self-abnegation, of which the whole range of thought admits.

All the humiliation and agony of the Saviour himself, were necessary to himself. Nothing less could have expressed the infinite love of the Divine nature; and in working out a most perfect righteousness for those he loved, he also wrought out a most perfect happiness for himself.

The eternal law of God links the happiness of all the creatures made in His image in an electric chain, united in the Divine love; and He, who has "a fellow-feeling for our infirmities," has given us a fellow-feeling with the sufferings of each other. So that no soul in which the Divine image is not totally obscured, can know of the misery of another, without a sympathetic throb of sorrow.

The true heart in Maine *cannot* know that the slave-mother in Georgia is weeping for her children, torn from her arms by avarice, without feeling her anguish palpitating in its inmost core.

It is the pulsations of the sympathetic heart which stretches out the hand to interfere between her and her aggressor; and abolitionists are just seeking a soft pillow, that they may "sleep o' nights."

It is selfishness, I tell you, all selfishness! The great whale when she gives up her own large life to protect her young one, and the little wren when she carries all the nice tit bits to her babies, are as true to themselves as the old pig when she shoulders all her little family out of the trough.

The whale enjoys death, and the wren her little fellows' supper, with a better zest than an old grunter does her corn, and Wm. Gildersten in spending money and laboring to prevent any more scenes of brutal violence in his State, by punishing the one past, gratifies his own loves and longings quite as much as Judge Grier in grunting out his wrath against all lovers of liberty.

The one would enjoy being hanged for the cause of God and Humanity, more than the other would the luxury of hanging him, even if he could have *all* the pleasure to himself,—be not only judge and persecutor, as he prefers, but marshal, jailor, and hangman to boot.

More than this, every creature, so far as other creatures are concerned, has a right to be happy in his own way. Nero had as much right to wish for power to cut off all the heads in Italy at one blow, as an innocent pig to wish for capacity to eat all the corn in the world. Mankind has no right to punish either for the desire or its manifestation, They should only make fences to prevent the accomplishment of the wish.

Americans have no right to punish Judge Grier for wishing to porsecute everybody who attempts to enforce State laws against murderous assaults by *his* officers. They should content themselves with fencing his Honor in, or, if necessary, putting a ring in his nose. He has as much right to be Judge Grier as George Washington had to be George Washington, and is no more selfish in following the instincts of his nature, than Washington was in following his.

Without any great respect,

I am your friend,

Jane G. Swisshelm

On Freedom.

ONCE I wished I might rehearse
Freedom's pæan in my verse,
That the slave who caught the strain
Should throb until he snapt his chain.
But the Spirit said, "Not so;
Speak it not, or speak it low;
Name not lightly to be said,
Gift too precious to be prayed,
Passion not to be exprest
But by heaving of the breast;
Yet,—would'st thou the mountain find
Where this deity is shrined,
Who gives the seas and sunset-skies
Their unspent beauty of surprise,
And, when it lists him, waken can
Brute and savage into man;

Or, if in thy heart he shine,
Blends the starry fates with thine,
Draws angels nigh to dwell with thee,
And makes thy thoughts archangels be ;
Freedom's secret would'st thou know ?—
Right thou feelest rashly do.

R. W. Emerson.

Mary Smith,

AN ANTI-SLAVERY REMINISCENCE.

SOME years ago a free colored woman, who was born in New England, and had gone to the south to attend upon some family, was shipwrecked, as she was returning northwards, on the coast of North Carolina. She, however, as well as some of the crew of the vessel, was saved. The half-civilized people of that region rendered some assistance to the shipwrecked party; but Mary Smith was detained by one of the natives as a slave.

The poor woman succeeded in getting a letter written to some person in Boston, in which the particulars of her story were narrated. Either this letter, or one afterwards written, contained references to people in Boston who were acquainted with her.

It was not very easy, even with these references, to get sufficient evidence to prove the freedom and identity of an obscure person, who had been away from Boston for some years. A strong interest, however, was felt in the case wherever it became known. And Rev. Samuel Snowden, well-remembered by the name of Father Snowden, with his usual indomitable energy and perseverance in aiding persons of his own color in distress, succeeded in finding people in Boston who were well acquainted with Mary Smith, and recollected her having left that place to go to the south. Pursuing his inquiries with great diligence, he ascertained the place of her birth, which was somewhere in New Hampshire. I forget the name of the town.

Affidavits were now procured, which established the place of Mary Smith's birth, her residence in Boston, and the time of her departure for the south, and other circumstances to corroborate her story.

Edward Everett, who was at this time Governor of Massachusetts, at the request of Mary Smith's friends, forwarded the documents they had obtained, accompanied with an urgent letter from himself, demanding her release from captivity, on the ground of her being a free citizen of Massachusetts.

The Governor of North Carolina replied very courteously to Governor Everett. He admitted the right of the woman to her freedom, and acknowledged that no person in North Carolina could lawfully detain her as a slave. But, at the same time he said, that as Governor, he had no power to interfere with the person who held her in custody. The decision on her right to freedom, depended on another department of the government. He promised, however, to write to the man who held her, and solicit her release.

The remonstrances of the Governor of North Carolina proved successful. Mary Smith soon arrived in Boston. And some of her old acquaintances who had given the evidence which led to her release, hastened to meet her and congratulate her on her escape from bondage. At the meeting they looked on her for some moments with astonishment, for they could trace in her features no resemblance to their former companion. A speedy explanation took place, from which it appeared that all the documents sent to North Carolina related to one Mary Smith; but the woman whose liberty they procured, was another Mary Smith.

Governor Everett had a hearty laugh when Father Snowden told him the happy result of his letter to the Governor of North Carolina.

The moral of this story is, that a plain, common name, is sometimes more useful to its owner, than a more brilliant one.

S. E. Sewall

NOTE.—I have endeavored to give the facts of Mary Smith's story with exact accuracy, writing from memory only, without the aid of anything written. It is possible I may be mistaken in some immaterial circumstance.

Freedom—Liberty.

FREEDOM and Liberty are synonymes. Freedom is an essence; Liberty, an accident. Freedom is born with a man; Liberty may be conferred on him. Freedom is progressive; Liberty is circumscribed. Freedom is the gift of God; Liberty, the creature of society. Liberty may be taken away from a man; but, on whatsoever soul Freedom may alight, the course of that soul is thenceforth onward and upward; society, customs, laws, armies, are but as wythes in its giant grasp, if they oppose, instruments to work its will, if they assent. Human kind welcome the birth of a free soul with reverence and shoutings, rejoicing in the advent of a fresh off-shoot of the Divine Whole, of which this is but a part.

James McCune Smith

NEW-YORK, Nov. 22d, 1853.

An Aspiration.

YOU want my autograph. Permit me, then, to sign myself the friend of every effort for human emancipation in our own country, and throughout the world. God speed the day when all chains shall fall from the limbs and from the soul, and universal liberty co-exist with universal righteousness and universal peace. In this work I am

Yours truly,

E. H. Chapin.

NEW YORK, Nov. 22d.

E. H. Chapin.

The Dying Soliloquy of the Victim of the Wilksbarre Tragedy.

"HE was approached from behind by Deputy Marshal Wyncoop and his assistants, knocked down with a mace and partially shackled. The fugitive, who had unsuspectingly waited upon them during their breakfast at the Phenix Hotel, was a tall, noble-looking, remarkably intelligent, and a nearly white mulatto; after a desperate effort and severe struggle, he shook off his *five* assailants, and with the loss of everything but a remnant of his shirt, rushed from the house and plunged into the water, exclaiming: "I will drown rather than be taken alive." He was pursued and fired upon several times, the last ball taking effect in his head, his face being instantly covered with blood. He sprang up and shrieked in great agony, and no doubt would have sunk at once, but for the buoyancy of the water. Seeing his condition, the slave-catchers retreated, coolly remarking that "dead niggers were not worth taking South."

Than be a slave,
Dread death I'll brave,
And hail the moment near,
When the soul mid pain,
Shall burst the chain
That long has bound it here.

Earth's thrilling pulse,
Man's stern repulse,
This weary heart no longer feels;
Its beating hushed
Its vain hopes crushed,
It craves that life which death reveals.

That moment great
My soul would wait,
In awe and peace sublime;
Nor bitter tears,
Nor slave-born fears,
As I pass from earth to time.

The angry past,
Like phantoms vast,
Glides by like the rushing wave;
So soon shall I,
Forgotten lie,
In the depths of my briny grave.

The time shall be,
"When no more sea"
Shall hide its treasures lone;
Then my soul shall rise,
Clothed for the skies,
To find its blissful home.

Foul deeds laid wrong
The whip and thong,
Have scored my manhood's heart,
But ne'er again
Shall fiends constrain
My body to the slave's vile mart.

The 'whelming wave,
This corpse shall lave;
Let the winds still pipe aloud,

Let the waters lash,
The white foam dash,
O'er my mangled brow and bloody shroud.

Roll on, thou free,
Unfettered sea,
Thy restless moan, my dirge,
My cradle deep
In my last lone sleep,
Is the scoop of thy hollow surge.

Would I might live,
One glance to give,
To those whose hearts would bless,
Each word of love,
All price above,
As mine to theirs I press.

The wish is vain ;
My frenzied brain,
Is dark'ning even now ;
Above, above,
Is Heaven's love,
And mercy's wide arched bow.

Glad free-born soul
With grateful hold,
Now grasp the gift from Heav'n—
Thy freedom won,
New life begun,
Forgive, thou'rt there forgiv'n.

H. H. Greenough

Let all be Free.

UNBOUNDED in thy expanse—far reaching
From shore to shore—ever beautiful
Are thy crystal waters—O sea.
Beautiful—when thy waves, the white pebbles lave,
When the weary sea-birds sleep, upon the bosom of
the deep.
But when thy storm-pressed billows burst,
The grasp which man would "lay upon thy mane,"
Then do I most love thee, sea,
Thou emblem of the *Free.*

When above me beam the stars,
How beautiful in their infinitude of light,
O'er the blue heavens spread, like gems
Upon the brow of youth!
Far, far away, beyond the paths of day,

More glorious yet, as suns which never set,
In darkness never! but shining forever!
You are more loved by me—
Ye emblems of the *Free.*

All earth of the beautiful is full.
Beautiful the streams which leave the rural vales,
Fringed with scarlet berries and leafy green!
O world of colors infinite, and lines of ever-varying
grace,
How by sea and shore art thou ever beautiful!
But the torrent rushing by, and the eagle in the sky,
The Alpine heights of snow where man does never go,
More lovely are to me,
For they are *Free.*

Beautiful is man, and yet more beautiful
Woman: coupled by bare circumstance
Of place or gold, still beautiful.
But this must fade!
Only the soul, grows never old:
They most agree, who most are free:
Liberty is the food of love!

The heavens, the earth, man's heart, and sea,
Forever cry, *let all be Free!*

C. M. Clay.

KENTUCKY, 1853.

Frederick Douglass

To the Editor of the "Autographs for Freedom."

DEAR MADAM,—

If the enclosed paragraph from a speech of mine delivered in May last, at the anniversary meeting of the American and Foreign Anti-Slavery Society, shall be deemed suited to the pages of the forthcoming annual, please accept it as my contribution.

With great respect,

Frederick Douglass,

ROCHESTER, November, 1853.

Extract.

NO colored man, with any nervous sensibility, can stand before an American audience without an intense and painful sense of the disadvantages imposed by his color. He feels little borne up by that brotherly sympathy and generous enthusiasm, which give wings to the eloquence, and strength to the hearts of other men, who advocate other and more popular causes. The ground which a colored man occupies in this country is, every inch of it, sternly disputed. Sir, were I a white man, speaking for the right of white men, I should in this country have a smooth sea and a fair wind. It is, perhaps, creditable to the American people (and I am not the man to detract from their credit) that they listen eagerly to the report of wrongs endured by distant nations. The Hungarian, the Italian, the Irishman, the Jew and the Gentile, all find in this goodly land a home; and when any of them, or all of them, desire to speak, they find willing ears, warm hearts, and open hands. For these people, the Americans have principles of justice, maxims of mercy, sentiments of religion, and feelings of brotherhood in abundance. But for *my* poor people, (alas, how poor!)—enslaved, scourged, blasted, overwhelmed, and ruined, it would appear that America had neither justice, mercy, nor religion. She has no scales in which to weigh our wrongs, and no standard by which to measure our rights. Just here lies the grand difficulty of the colored man's cause. It is found in the fact, that we may not avail ourselves of the just force of admitted American principles. If I do not misinterpret the feelings and philosophy of my white fellow-countrymen generally, they wish us to understand distinctly and fully that they have no other use for us whatever, than to coin dollars out of our blood.

Our position here is anomalous, unequal, and extraordinary. It is a position to which the most courageous of our race cannot look without deep concern. Sir, we are a hopeful people, and in this we are fortunate; but for this trait of our character, we should have, long before this seemingly unpropitious hour, sunk down under a sense of utter despair.

Look at it, sir. Here, upon the soil of our birth, in a country which has known us for two centuries, among a people who did not wait for us to seek them, but who sought us, found us, and brought us to their own chosen land,—a people for whom we have performed the humblest services, and whose greatest comforts and luxuries have been won from the soil by our sable and sinewy arms,—I say, sir, among such a people, and with such obvious recommendations to favor, we are far less esteemed than the veriest stranger and sojourner.

Aliens are we in our native land. The fundamental principles of the republic, to which the humblest white man, whether born here or elsewhere, may appeal with confidence in the hope of awakening a favorable response, are held to be inapplicable to us. The glorious doctrines of your revolutionary fathers, and the more glorious teachings of the Son of God, are construed and applied against us. We are literally scourged beyond the beneficent range of both authorities,—human and divine. We plead for our rights, in the name of the immortal declaration of independence, and of the written constitution of government, and we are answered with imprecations and curses. In the sacred name of Jesus we beg for mercy, and the slave-whip, red with blood, cracks over us in mockery. We invoke the aid of the ministers of Him who came "to preach deliverance to the captive," and to set at liberty them that are bound, and from the loftiest summits of this ministry comes the inhuman and blasphemous response, saying: if one prayer would move the Almighty arm in mercy to break your galling chains, that prayer would be withheld. We cry for help to humanity—a common humanity, and here too we are repulsed. American humanity hates us, scorns us, disowns and denies, in a thousand ways, our very personality. The outspread wing of American Christianity, apparently broad enough to give shelter to a perishing world, refuses to cover us. To us, its bones are brass, and its feathers iron. In running thither for shelter and succor, we have only fled from the hungry bloodhound to the devouring wolf,—from a corrupt and selfish world to a hollow and hypocritical church.

Extract from an unpublished Poem on Freedom.

OH, Freedom! when thy morning march began,
Coëval with the birth and breath of man;
Who that could view thee in that Asian clime,
God-born, soul-nursed, the infant heir of time—
Who that could see thee in that Asian court,
Flit with the sparrow, with the lion sport,
Talk with the murmur of the babbling rill
And sing thy summer song upon the hill—
Who that could know thee as thou wast inwrought
The all in all of nature's primal thought,
And see thee given by Omniscient mind,
A native boon to lord, and brute, and wind,
Could e'er have dreamed with fate's prophetic sleep,
The darker lines thy horoscope would keep,
Or trembling read, thro' tones with horror thrilled,
The damned deeds thy future name would gild?

Lo! The swart chief of Afric's vergeless plains,
Poor Heaven-wept child of nature's joys and pains,
Mounts his fleet steed with wind-directed course,
Nor checks again his free unbridled horse,
But lordless, wanders where his will inclines
From Tuats heats to Zegzeg's stunted pines!
View him, ye craven few, ye living-dead!
Wrecks of a being whence the soul has fled!
Ye Goths and Vandals of his plundered coast!
Ye *christian* Bondous, who of feeling boast,*
Who quickly kindling to historic fire
Contemn a Marius' or a Scylla's ire,†

* "Ye Christian *Bondous* who of feeling boast!"

Unable in the whole range of my vernacular, to find an epithet sufficiently expressive to enunciate the aggravated contempt which all feel for that pseudonymous class of philanthropists, who flauntingly parade a pompous sympathy with popular and distant distresses, but studiously cultivate a coarse ignorance of, and hauteur to, the Greeks, which "are at the door," I have had recource to the Metonymy, *Bondou*, as rendered mournfully significant through the melancholy fate of the illustrious Houghton.—Vide *Report African Discovery Society.*

† "Contemn a Marius' or a Scylla's ire."

Napoleon in his protest to Lord Bathurst, provoked by the petty tyranny of Sir Hudson Lowe, said of the "Proscriptions," and (by negative inference) in extenuation of them, that they "*were made with the blood yet fresh upon the sword.*" A sentence, which, falling from the lips of one of the most imperturbably cool and calculating of mankind, under circumstances superinducing peculiar reflection on every word uttered, cannot but come with the force of a whole volume of excoria-

Or kindly lulled to sympathetic glow,
Lament the martyrs of some far-off woe,
And tender grown, with sorrow hugely great,
Weep o'er an Agis' or Jugurtha's fate ! *
View him, ye hollow heartlings as he stalks
The dauntless monarch of his native walks
Breathes the warm odor which the girgir bears,†

tive evidence against the demoralization of war, even upon the most abstracted and elevated natures.—Vide *Letters of Montholon and Las Cases.*

* "Weep o'er an Agis' or Jugurtha's fate."

Agis, King of Lacedemon and colleague of Leonidas, was a youth of singular purity and promise. Aiming to correct the abuses which had crept into the Spartan polity, he introduced regenerative laws. Among others, one for the equalization of property, and as an example of disinterested liberality, shared his estate with the community. Unappreciated by the degenerated Senate however, he was deposed, and, with his whole family, strangled by order of the ingrate State.—*Edin. Encyc.*

It is said that when Jugurtha was led before the car of the conquerer, he lost his senses. After the triumph he was thrown into prison, where, whilst they were in haste to strip him, some tore his robes off his back, and others, catching eagerly at his pendants, pulled off the tips of his ears with them. When he was thrust down naked into the dungeon, all wild and confused, he said, with a frantic smile, "Heavens ! how cold is this bath of yours !" There struggling for six days with starvation, and to the last hour laboring for the preservation of his life, he came to his end.—*Plut. Cai. Mar.*

† "Breathes the warm odor which the *girgir* bears."

The girgir, or the *geshe el aube*, a species of flowering grass. Piercing, fragrant, and grateful in its odor, it operates not unlike a mild stimulant, when respired for any length of time, and is found chiefly near the borders of small streams and in the vicinage of the Tassada.—*Lyn. Gui. and Soud.*

Shouts the fierce music of his savage airs,
Or madly brave in hottest chase pursues
The tawny monster of the desert dews;
Eager, erect, persistent as the storm,
Soul in his mien, God's image in his form!
Yes, view him thus, from Kaffir to Soudan,
And tell me, worldlings, is the black a man?

See, the full sun emerging from the deep,
Climbs with red eye, the light-illumined steep,
And brightly beautiful continuous smiles
A fecund blessing on those Indian Isles!
Like eastern woods which sweeten as they burn,
So, the parched earths to odorous flowrets turn,
And feathered fayes their murmurous wings expand,
Waked by the magic of his conjuror's wand,
Flash their red plumes, and vocalize each dell
Where browse the fecho and the dun-gazelle,*

* "Where browse the *fecho* and the dun-gazelle."

Among the wild animals are prodigious numbers of the vari-colored species of the gazelle, the bohur sassa, fecho, and madoqua. They are extremely numerous in the provinces depopulated *by war and slavery,* enjoying the wild oats of the deserted hamlets without fear of molestation from a returning population.—*Notes on Central Africa.*

While half forgetful of her changing sphere,
The loathful summer lingers year by year.
Here, in the light of God's supernal eye—
His realms unbounded, and his woes a sigh—
The dusky son of evening placed whileome
Found with the Gnu an ever-vernal home,
And wiser than Athenas' wisest schools,*
Nor led by zealots, nor scholastic rules,
Gazed at the stars that stud yon tender blue,
And hoped, and deemed the cheat of death untrue;

* "And wiser than Athenas' wisest schools,
Nor led by zealots, nor scholastic rules,
Gazed at the stars which stud yon tender blue,
And hoped and deemed the cheat of death untrue."

Though Socrates and Plato, particularly the former, are generally admitted by writers of authority, among whom, indeed, are Polycarpe, Chrysotom, and Eusebius, to have in a manner *suspected* rather than believed, the immortality of the soul; yet we have no evidence of their ever having, by the finest process of ratiocination, so thoroughly convinced themselves as to introduce it generally as a tenable thesis on the portico. A beautiful thread of implicit belief and fervent hope, of after life, assimilating to the hunting-ground of our own American Indians, and though sensuous still, a step far in advance of the black void of ancient philosophy, has always run through the higher mythologies of the Negro. So notorious, indeed, was the fact among early Christians, that that ubiquitous riddle, "Prestor John," was, by believers, regarded as naving a *locale* in Central Africa; while Henry of Portugal actually despatched two ambassadors, Corvilla and Payvan, to a rumored Christian court, south of the Sahara.—*Edin. Encyc. Early Chris. His. Port.*

Yet, supple sophist to a plastic mind*
Saw gods in woods, and spirits in the wind,
Heard in the tones that stirred the waves within,
The mingled voice of Hadna and Odin,
Doomed the fleeced tenant of the wild to bleed
A guileless votive to his harmless creed,
Then gladly grateful at each rite fulfilled,
Sought the cool shadow where the spring distilled,
And lightly lab'rous thro' the torpid day,
Whiled in sweet peace the sultry eve away.

Or if perchance to nature darkly true,
He strikes the war-path thro' the midnight dew,
Steals in the covert on the sleeping foe,
And wreaks the horrors of a barbarous woe;
Yet, yet returning to the home-girt spot—

* "Yet supple sophist to a plastic mind,
Sees gods in woods, and spirits in the wind."

The imagination of the African, like his musical genius, which extracts surprising harmony from the rudest of sources, the clapping of hands, the clanking of chains, the resonance of lasso wood, and perforated shells, seems to invest everything with a resident spirit of peculiar power. Accordingly, his mythologies are most numerous and poetical—his entire catalogue of superior gods alone, embracing a more extended length than the Assyro-Babylon Alphabet, with its three hundred letters.

The vengeful causes and the deed forgot—*
Where greenest boughs o'er sloping banks impend,
And gurgling waves to bosky dells descend;
Intent the long expectant brood to sea,
He halts beneath the broad acacia tree;
And warmly pressed by wonder-gloating eyes,
Displays the vantage of each savage prize;
Stills with glad pride and plundered gems, uncouth,
The ardent longings of his daughter's youth;

Bids the dark spouse the tropic meal prepare,
Mid laughing echoes from the bird-voiced air;
Passes before him in a fond review
The merry numbers of his crisp-haired crew;†

* "The vengeful causes and the deed forgot."

All travellers agree in the facile ductility and inertia-like amiability of the native African character.—BREWSTER *on Africa.*

† "The merry numbers of his crisp-haired crew."

The negro race is, perhaps, the most prolific of all the human species. Their infancy and youth are singularly happy. The parents are passionately fond of their children.—GOLDBURY'S *Travels.*

"Strike me," said my attendant, "but do not curse my mother." The same sentiment I found universally to prevail.

Some of the first lessons in which the Mandings women instruct their children is the *practice of truth.* It was the only consolation for a negro mother, whose son had been murdered by the Moors, that "*the boy had never told a lie.*"—PARK'S *Travels.*

Recounts the dangers of the last night's strife,
Joys with their joy, and lives their inner life;
And then when slow the lengthened day expires,
Mid twilight balms and star-enkindled fires,
With *all* the father sees each form retire,
A ruthless heathen, but a loving sire.*

Innocuously thus, thro' long, long years
Untaught by learning, yet unknown to fears,
The swarthy Afric whiled the jocund hours,
A petted child of nature's rosiest bowers,
Till lured by wealth the hardy Portuguese,†
Seeks the green waters of his Eastern seas,

* "With all the father sees each form retire,
A ruthless heathen, but a loving sire."

"Or led the combat, bold without a plan,
An artless savage, but a fearless man."
CAMPBELL.

† "Till lured by wealth the hardy Portuguese,
Sought the green waters of his Eastern seas,
And venturous nations more excursive grown,
Pierced his glad coast from radiant zone to zone."

Vasquez de Gama, a Portuguese nobleman, was the first to discover a maritime passage to the Indies; unless, perhaps, we credit the improbable achievement of the Phœnicians, related by Herodotus as occurring, 604 B.C.

De Gama doubled the cape in 1498, explored the eastern shores as far as Melinda, in Zanguebar, and sailing thence arrived at Calcutta in May. This expedition, second to none in its results, save that of

And venturous nations more excursive grown,
Scan his glad coast from radiant zone to zone,
Then Fortune's minion in a foreign clime,
Cursed by his own and damned to later time,
Of incest born and by the chances thrown
A tainted alien on a ravished throne,
Gapes the foul flatteries of a fawning train,
And fatuous mock'ries, which themselves disdain,
A fancied monarch, but the witless sport
Of adulation, and a practiced court,
Vaunts to his broad realms and Timour-like proclaims
Illusive titles of barbaric names,
Cheats his own nature, and now generous grown,*

Columbus six years before, drew the attention of all Europe. Whole nations became actuated by the same enthusiasm, and private companies of merchants sent out whole fleets on voyages of discovery, scouring the entire coast from Cape Verd to Gaudfui, and discovering the Mascharenhas and most of the islands of the Ethiopean Archipelago.

* "Cheats his own nature and now generous grown,
Dispenses realms and empires not his own."

Charles V. granted a patent *to one of his Flemish favorites*, containing an exclusive right to import four thousand negroes!—*Hist. Slavery.*

The crime of having *first* recommended the importation of African slaves into America, *is due to the Flemish nobility*, who obtained a monopoly of four thousand negroes, which they sold to some Genoese merchants for 25,000 ducats.—*Life of Cardinal Ximenes.*

They (the Genoese) were the first to bring into a regular form,

Dispenses souls and empires not his own,
Draws the deep purple round his royal seat,
Lifts his low crest, affects the God complete,
By giving with light breath, oh, shame to tell!
These heirs of Heav'n unto the fate of hell.
Sped by the mandate of his recreant train,
Lo! commerce, broad winged seraph of the main!
Shook her white plumage and coqueting, won
Propitious favors from the southern sun,
Till manly hearts and keel-impelling gales,
Furled on the coast her half-reluctant sails.

Abashed, amazed, with fear-dilated eye
The marvelling tribes these new-born wonders spy;
See from the shore, bright glittering in the sun,
The moving freightage of each galleon;
Wait till the measured strokes of oars bring near
These way-lost wanderers of another sphere,
Then timorously glad, yet awe-struck still,
Lead from the sunshine to the breezy hill;
With courteous grace a resting place assign
'Neath rustling leaves and grape-empurpled vine,

that commerce for slaves, between Africa and America, which has since grown to such an amazing extent.—*Robertson.*

And led by craft in artless pride make known
The lustrous lurements of their gorgeous zone,
As in the field some skilful ranger sets
The fraudful cordage of his specious nets,
Places some fragrant viand in the snare,
And captive takes the unsuspicious hare;
So the bold strangers with superior will
Lay their base plans with disingenuous skill,
Ope their stored treasures and with art display
Their worthless figments to the air of day,
Roll their large lids, and with grave gestures laud
Each tinsel trinket and each painted gaud;
With mystic signs of strange import apply
Some gew-gaw bauble to the gloating eye;
Touch with nice skill, yet craft-dissembled smile,
Gems from the mine and spices from the Isle,
Affect no care, yet hope a thrifty sale—
The wealth of Empires in th' opposing scale—
While he, the poor victim of their selfish creed,
Prescient of evil art foredoomed to bleed,
Pleased yet alarmed, desiring but deterred,
Flutters still nearer like a snake-charmed bird;
Alas, too often taken with a toy—
Too soon to weep a kindred fate with Troy!

Evils received, like twilight stars dilate,
The less the light, the larger grows their state;
Thus the first error in that savage air,
Spreads as a flame, and leaves a ruin there.
Too dearly generous and too warmly true,*
The simple black wears out the fatal clew,—
From barter flies to trade; from trade to wants;
From wants to interests and derided haunts;
Thence, rolls from off the once-sequestered shore,
The turgid tide of havoc and of war;
No warning ringing from the red adunes,
No prophets rising, and no Laocoons,
Remotest tribes the baleful influence own;
Feel to extremes, and at their centres groan.
Now laughs the stranger at their anguished throes,†
Feeds on their ills, and battens on their woes;

* "Too warmly generous and dearly true,
The simple black," &c.

It will remain an indelible reproach on the name of Europeans, that for more than three centuries their intercourse with the Africans has only tended to destroy their happiness and debase their character.—*Edin. Ency.*

† "Now laughs the stranger at their anguished throes."

The arts of the slave-merchant have inflamed the hostility of their various tribes, and heightened their ferocity by sedulously increasing their wars.—*Ibid.*

Glads his freed conscience at each pillaged mine,
And finds forgiveness at a Christian shrine;
By specious creeds and sophists darkly taught,*
To semble virtue and dissemble thought,
With Saviour-seeming smile, adds fuel to the flame,—
Ulysses' craft, without Ulysses' aim,—
And sadly faithful to his dark designs,
Fiction improves; heroic rage refines;
For lo! Achilles, victor of the train!
Draws Hector lifeless, round the Ilian plain;
But ah! these later Greeks more cruel strive,
And bind their victim to the load alive!

Oh, beats there, Heaven, beneath thy gorgeous blue,
One heart so basely to itself untrue,
So dead of pulse, and so insensate grown,
It feels not such a cause dear as its own?

* "By specious creeds and sophists darkly taught."

Hamlet's advice to his offending mother;—

"Assume a virtue, tho' you have it not."

Adding hypocrisy to avowed unworthiness, was the acknowledged injunction of the church, wherever and whenever she participated in secular affairs, with a view of emolument. For a peculiar illustration of this favorite doctrine, see Clement VI.'s edict, when, in virtue of the right arrogated by the holy see *to dispose of all countries belonging to the heathen*, he erected (1344) the Canaries into a kingdom, and disposed of them to Lewis de la Corda, a prince of Castile.

Dwells there a being 'neath thine eye, oh, God!
A fellow-worm from out the self-same clod,
Whose fevered blood does not impatient boil,
Fierce as a tiger's in the hunter's toil,
To see degenerate men and States prolong,
So foul a deed—so thrice accursed a wrong?
Tell me, ye loud-voiced winds that ceaseless roll,
Eternal miracles from pole to pole,
Breathes there on earth so vile and mean a thing
That crushed, it will not turn again and sting?
And say! ye tyrants in your boasted halls,
Read ye no warnings on your darkened walls?
Hear ye no seeming mutterings of the cloud
Break from the millions which your steps have bowed?
Think ye, ye hold in your ignoble thrall,
Mind, soul, thought, taste, hope, feeling, valor, all?
No; these unfettered scorn your nerveless hand,
Sport at their will, and scoff at your command,
Range through arcades of shadow-brooding palms,
Snuff their free airs and breathe their floating balms,
Or bolder still, on fancy's fiery wing—*

* "Or bolder still on fancy's fiery wing."

That I do not exaggerate the *belle lettres* and classical accomplishments of at least two of the "chattels" of the "peculiar institution," in the lines following the above, see "Poems written by Rosa and Maria," *property* of South Carolina, and published in 1834.

Caught from their letters at the noon-day spring—
With star-eyed science, and her seraph train
Read the bright secrets of yon azure plain;
Hear Loxian murmurs in Rhodolphe's caves*
Meet with sweet answers from the nymph-voiced
waves;
Sit with the pilot at Phœnicia's helm,
And mark the boundries of the Lybian realm;
See swarthy Memnon in the grave debate,
Dispute with gods, and rule a conqu'ring state,
And warmly and kindling dare—yes, *dare* to hope,
A second Empire on the future's scope!

And thou, my country, latest born of time!
Dearest of all, of all the most sublime!
How long shall patriots own, with blush of shame,
So foul a blot upon so fair a name?
How long thy sons with filial hearts deplore,
A Python evil on thy Cyprean shore?

* "Hear *Loxian* murmurs in Rodolphe's caves."

Loxian is a name frequently given to Apollo by Greek writers, and is met with, more than once, in the "Chœphoræ of Eschylus." —*Campbell.*

Euripides mentions it three times, and Sophocles twice, its euphony recommends it more than any other name of the fair-haired god.

What! and wilt thou, the moral Hercules
Whose youth eclipsed the dream of Pericles,
Whose trunceant bands heroically caught,
The Spartan phalanx with the Attic thought,
The wizard throne of age-nursed error hurled,
Defied a tyrant and transfixed a world!
Wilt *thou* see Afric like old Priam sue,
The bones of children as in nature due,
And foully craven, ingrate-like forget,
Thy life, thy learning's her dishonored debt?
Say; wilt not *thou*, whose time-ennobling sons—
Thy Jay's, thy Franklin's and thy Washington's,
Caught the bright cestus from fair freedom's God,
And bound it as a girdle to thy sod;
Ah! wilt not thou with generous mind confess
The might of woe, the strength of helplessness?
High-Heaven's almoner to a world oppressed,
Who in the march of nations led the rest! *
Will there no Gracchus in *thy* Senate stand
And speak the words that millions should command?
No Clysthementhe 'neath thy broad arched dome,
Predict the fortunes with the crimes of Rome?

* "And in the march of nations led the *van*."
Campbell.

Shall time yet partial in his cycling course,
Bring thee no Fox, no Pitt, no Wilberforce?
Still must thou live and corybantic die,
A traceless meteor in a clouding sky;
Thy name a cheat; thyself, a world-wide lie?
No; there will come, prophetic hearts may trust,
Some embryo angel of superior dust,
With brow of cloud and tongue of livid flame—
Another Moses, but in time and name—
Whose Heaven-appealing voice shall bid thee pass—
On either hand a wall of living glass;—
Ope for the Lybian with convulsive shock
His more than Horeb's adamantine rock,
And gazing from some second Pisgah, see
Thy idol broken and thy people free.

William D. Snow.

RICHMOND, Dec. 1st, 1853.

Letter

BROOKLYN, December 6th, 1853.

DEAR SIR,—

Your note of November 29th, requesting a line from me for the Autographs for Freedom, is received.

I wish that I had something that would add to the literary value of your laudable enterprise. In so great a cause as that of human liberty, every great interest in society ought to have a voice and a decisive testimony. Art should be in sympathy with freedom and literature, and all human learning should speak with *unmistakable* accents for the elevation, evangelization, and liberation of the oppressed. In a future day, the historian cannot purge our political history from the shame of wanton and mercenary oppression. But there is not, I believe, a book in the literature of our country that will be alive and known a hundred years hence, in which can be found the taint of despotism. The literature of the world is on the side of liberty.

I am very truly yours.

Henry Ward Beecher

H B Stowe

PLAYFORD HALL, SUFFOLK. The seat of Thomas Clarkson, Esq

A Day spent at Playford Hall.

IT was a pleasant morning in May,—I believe that is the orthodox way of beginning a story,—when C. and I took the cars to go into the country to Playford Hall. "And what's Playford Hall?" you say. "And why did you go to see it?" As to what it is, here is a reasonably good picture before you. As to why, it was for many years the residence of Thomas Clarkson, and is now the residence of his venerable widow and her family.

Playford Hall is considered, I think, the oldest of the fortified houses in England, and is, I am told, the only one that has water in the moat. The water which is seen girdling the wall in the picture, is the moat; it surrounds the place entirely, leaving no access except across the bridge, which is here represented.

After crossing this bridge, you come into a green court-yard, filled with choice plants and flowering shrubs, and carpeted with that thick, soft, velvet-like grass, which is to be found nowhere else in so perfect a state as in England.

The water is fed by a perpetual spring, whose current is so sluggish as scarcely to be perceptible, but which yet has the vitality of a running stream.

It has a dark and glassy stillness of surface, only broken by the forms of the water plants, whose leaves float thickly over it.

The walls of the moat are green with ancient moss, and from the crevices springs an abundant flowering vine, whose delicate leaves and bright yellow flowers in some places entirely mantled the stones with their graceful drapery.

The picture I have given you represents only one side of the moat. The other side is grown up with dark and thick shrubbery and ancient trees, rising and embowering the whole place, adding to the retired and singular effect of the whole. The place is a specimen of a sort of thing which does not exist in America. It is one of those significant landmarks which unite the present with the past, for which we must return to the country of our origin.

Playford Hall is a thing peculiarly English, and Thomas Clarkson, for whose sake I visited it, was as peculiarly an Englishman,—a specimen of the very best kind of English mind and character, as this is of characteristic English architecture.

We Anglo-Saxons have won a hard name in the world. There are undoubtedly bad things which are true about us.

Taking our developments as a race, both in England and America, we may be justly called the Romans of the nineteenth century. We have been the race which has conquered, subdued, and broken in pieces, other weaker races, with little regard either to justice or mercy. With regard to benefits by us imparted to conquered nations, I think a better story, on the whole, can be made out for the Romans than for us. Witness the treatment of the Chinese, of the tribes of India, and of our own American Indians.

But still there is an Anglo-Saxon blood, a vigorous sense of justice, as appears in our Habeas Corpus, our jury trials, and other features of State organization, and, when this is tempered in individuals, with the elements of gentleness and compassion, and enforced by that energy and indomitable perseverance which are characteristic of the Anglo-Saxon mind, they form a style of philanthropists peculiarly efficient. In short, the Anglo-Saxon is efficient, in whatever he sets himself about, whether in crushing the weak, or lifting them up.

Thomas Clarkson was born in a day when good, pious people, imported cargoes of slaves from Africa, as one of the regular Christianized modes of gaining a subsistence, and providing for them and their households. It was a thing that everybody was doing, and everybody thought they had a right to do. It was supposed that all the coffee, tea, and sugar in the world were dependent on stealing men, women, and children, and could be got no other way; and as to consume coffee, sugar, rice, and rum, were evidently the chief ends of human existence, it followed that men, women, and children, must be stolen to the end of time.

Some good people, when they now and then heard an appalling story of the cruelties practiced in the slave ship, declared that it was really too bad, sympathetically remarked, "What a sorrowful world we live in," stirred their sugar into their tea, and went on as before, because, what was there to do—hadn't everybody always done it, and if they didn't do it, wouldn't somebody else?

It is true that for many years individuals, at different times, remonstrated, had written treatises, poems, stories, and movements had been made by some religious ladies, particularly the Quakers, but the opposition had amounted to nothing practically efficient.

The attention of Clarkson was first turned to the subject by having it given out as the theme for a prize composition in his college class, he being at that time a sprightly young man, about twenty-four years of age. He entered into the investigation with no other purpose than to see what he could make of it as a college theme.

He says of himself: "I had expected pleasure from the invention of arguments, from the arrangement of them, from the putting of them together, and from the thought, in the interim, that I was engaged in an innocent contest for literary honor, but all my pleasures were damped by the facts, which were now continually before me.

"It was but one gloomy subject from morning till

night; in the day time I was uneasy, in the night I had little rest, I sometimes never closed my eyelids for grief."

It became not now so much a trial for academical reputation as to write a work which should be useful to Africa. It is not surprising that a work, written under the force of such feelings, should have gained the prize, as it did. Clarkson was summoned from London to Cambridge, to deliver his prize essay publicly. He says of himself, on returning back to London: "The subject of it almost wholly engrossed my thoughts. I became at times very seriously affected while on the road. I stopped my horse occasionally, dismounted, and walked.

"I frequently tried to persuade myself that the contents of my essay could not be true, but the more I reflected on the authorities on which they were founded, the more I gave them credit. Coming in sight of Wade's Mill, in Hertfordshire, I sat down disconsolate on the turf by the roadside, and held my horse. Here a thought came into my mind, that if the contents of the essay were true, it was time that somebody should see these calamities to an end."

These reflections, as it appears, were put off for awhile, but returned again.

This young and noble heart was of a kind that could not comfort itself so easily for a brother's sorrow as many do.

He says of himself: "In the course of the autumn of the same year, I walked frequently into the woods that I might think of the subject in solitude, and find relief to my mind there; but there the question still recurred, 'are these things true?' Still the answer followed as instantaneously, 'they are;' still the result accompanied it,—surely some person should interfere. I began to envy those who had seats in Parliament, riches, and widely-extended connections, which would enable them to take up this cause.

"Finding scarcely any one, at the time, who thought of it, I was turned frequently to myself, but here many difficulties arose. It struck me, among others, that a young man only twenty-four years of age could not have that solid judgment, or that knowledge of men, manners, and things, which were requisite to qualify him to undertake a task of such magnitude and importance; and with whom was I to unite? I believed, also, that it looked so much like one of the feigned labors of Hercules, that my understanding would be suspected, if I proposed it."

He however resolved to do something for the cause by translating his essay from Latin into English, enlarging and presenting it to the public. Immediately on the publication of this essay, he discovered to his astonishment and delight, that he was not the only one who had been interested in this subject.

Being invited to the house of William Dillwyn, one of these friends to the cause, he says: "How surprised was I to learn, in the course of our conversation, of the labors of Granville Sharp, of the writings of Ramsey, and of the controversy in which the latter was engaged, of all which I had hitherto known nothing. How surprised was I to learn that William Dillwyn had, himself, two years before, associated himself with five others for the purpose of enlightening the public mind on this great subject.

"How astonished was I to find, that a society had been formed in America for the same object. These thoughts almost overpowered me. My mind was overwhelmed by the thought, that I had been providentially directed to this house; the finger of Providence was beginning to be discernible, and that the day-star of African liberty was rising."

After this he associated with many friends of the cause, and at last it became evident that in order to effect anything, he must sacrifice all other prospects in life, and devote himself exclusively to this work.

He says, after mentioning reasons which prevented all his associates from doing this: "I could look, therefore, to no person but myself; and the question was, whether I was prepared to make the sacrifice. In favor of the undertaking, I urged to myself that never was any cause, which had been taken up by man, in any country or in any age, so great and important; that never was there one in which so much misery was heard to cry for redress; that never was there one in which so much good could be done; never one in which the duty of christian charity could be so extensively exercised; never one more worthy of the devotion of a whole life towards it; and that, if a man thought properly, he ought to rejoice to have been called into existence, if he were only permitted to become an instrument in forwarding it in any part of its progress.

"Against these sentiments, on the other hand, I had

to urge that I had been designed for the church; that I had already advanced as far as deacon's orders in it; that my prospects there on account of my connections were then brilliant; that, by appearing to desert my profession, my family would be dissatisfied, if not unhappy. These thoughts pressed upon me, and rendered the conflict difficult.

"But the sacrifice of my prospects staggered me, I own, the most. When the other objections which I have related, occurred to me, my enthusiasm instantly, like a flash of lightning, consumed them; but this stuck to me, and troubled me. I had ambition. I had a thirst after worldly interest and honors, and I could not extinguish it at once. I was more than two hours in solitude under this painful conflict. At length I yielded, not because I saw any reasonable prospect of success in my new undertaking, for all cool-headed and cool-hearted men would have pronounced against it; but in obedience, I believe, to a higher Power. And I can say, that both on the moment of this resolution, and for some time afterwards, I had more sublime and happy feelings than at any former period of my life."

In order to show how this enterprise was looked

upon and talked of very commonly by the majority of men in these times, we will extract the following passage from Boswell's Life of Johnson, in which Bozzy thus enters his solemn protest: "The wild and dangerous attempt, which has for some time been persisted in, to obtain an act of our Legislature, to abolish so very important and necessary a branch of commercial interest, must have been crushed at once, had not the insignificance of the zealots, who vainly took the lead in it, made the vast body of planters, merchants and others, whose immense properties are involved in that trade, reasonably enough suppose, that there could be no danger. The encouragement which the attempt has received, excites my wonder and indignation; and though some men of superior abilities have supported it, whether from a love of temporary popularity, when prosperous; or a love of general mischief, when desperate, my opinion is unshaken.

"To abolish a statute which in all ages God has sanctioned, and man has continued, would not only be robbery to an innumerable class of our fellow-subjects, but it would be extreme cruelty to the African savages, a portion of whom it saves from massacre, or intolerable bondage in their own country, and introduces into a much happier state of life; especially now, when their passage to the West Indies, and their treatment there, is humanely regulated. To abolish this trade, would be to

'—— shut the gates of mercy on mankind.'"

One of the first steps of Clarkson and his associates, was the formation of a committee of twelve persons, for the collection and dissemination of evidence on the subject.

The contest now began in earnest, a contest as sublime as any the world ever saw.

The Abolition controversy more fully aroused the virtue, the talent, and the religion of the great English nation, than any other event or crisis which ever occurred.

Wilberforce was the leader of the question in Parliament. The other members of the Anti-slavery Committee performed those labors which were necessary out of it.

This labor consisted principally in the collection of evidence with regard to the traffic, and the presentation of it before the public mind. In this labor

Clarkson was particularly engaged. The subject was hemmed in with the same difficulties that now beset the Anti-slavery cause in America. Those who knew most about it, were precisely those whose interest it was to prevent inquiry. An immense moneyed interest was arrayed against investigation, and was determined to suppress the agitation of the subject. Owing to this powerful pressure, many who were in possession of facts which would bear upon this subject, refused to communicate them; and often after a long and wearisome journey in search of an individual who could throw light upon the subject, Clarkson had the mortification to find his lips sealed by interest or timidity. As usual, the cause of oppression was defended by the most impudent lying; the slave-trade was asserted to be the latest revised edition of philanthropy. It was said that the poor African, the slave of miserable oppression in his own country, was wafted by it to an asylum in a Christian land; that the middle passage was to the poor negro a perfect elysium, infinitely happier than anything he had ever known in his own country. All this was said while manacles, and hand-cuffs, and thumb-screws, and instruments to force open the mouth, were a regular part of the stock for a slave ship, and were hanging in the shop windows of Liverpool for sale.

For Clarkson's attention was first called to these things by observing them in the shop window, and on inquiring the use of one of them, the man informed him that many times negroes were sulky and tried to starve themselves to death, and this instrument was used to force open their jaws.

Of Clarkson's labor in this investigation some idea may be gathered from his own words, when stating that for a season he was compelled to retire from the cause, he thus speaks. "As far as I myself was concerned, all exertion was then over. The nervous system was almost shattered to pieces. Both my memory and my hearing failed me. Sudden dizzinesses seized my head. A confused singing in the ear followed me wherever I went. On going to bed the very stairs seemed to dance up and down under me, so that, misplacing my foot, I sometimes fell. Talking, too, if it continued but half an hour, exhausted me so that profuse perspirations followed, and the same effect was produced even by an active exertion of the mind for the like time.

These disorders had been brought on by degrees, in

consequence of the severe labors necessarily attached to the promotion of the cause. For seven years I had a correspondence to maintain with four hundred persons, with my own hand; I had some book or other annually to write in behalf of the cause. In this time I had traveled more than thirty-five thousand miles in search of evidence, and a great part of these journeys in the night. All this time my mind had been on the stretch. It had been bent too to this one subject, for I had not even leisure to attend to my own concerns. The various instances of barbarity which had come successively to my knowledge within this period, had vexed, harrassed, and afflicted it. The wound which these had produced was rendered still deeper by those cruel disappointments before related, which arose from the reiterated refusals of persons to give their testimony, after I had traveled hundreds of miles in quest of them. But the severest stroke was that inflicted by the persecution, begun and pursued by persons interested in the continuance of the trade, of such witnesses as had been examined against them; and whom, on account of their dependent situation in life, it was most easy to oppress. As I had been the means of bringing these forward on these occasions, they naturally came to me, when thus persecuted, as the author of their miseries and their ruin. From their supplications and wants it would have been ungenerous and ungrateful to have fled. These different circumstances, by acting together, had at length brought me into the situation just mentioned; and I was therefore obliged, though very reluctantly, to be borne out of the field, where I had placed the great honor and glory of my life."

I may as well add here that a Mr. Whitbread, to whom Clarkson mentioned this latter cause of distress, generously offered to repair the pecuniary losses of all who had suffered in this cause. One anecdote will be a specimen of the energy with which Clarkson pursued evidence. It had been very strenuously asserted and maintained that the subjects of the slave trade were only such unfortunates as had become prisoners of war, and who, if not carried out of the country in this manner, would be exposed to death or some more dreadful doom in their own country. This was one of those stories which nobody believed, and yet was particularly useful in the hands of the opposition, because it was difficult legally to disprove it. It was perfectly well known that in very many cases slave-traders made direct incursions into the country, kidnapped, and carried off the inhabitants of whole villages, but the question was, how to establish it? A gentleman whom Clarkson accidentally met on one of his journeys, informed him that he had been in company, about a year before, with a sailor, a very respectable looking young man, who had actually been engaged in one of these expeditions; he had spent half an hour with him at an inn; he described his person, but knew nothing of his name or the place of his abode, all he knew was that he belonged to a ship of war in ordinary, but knew nothing of the port. Clarkson determined that this man should be produced as a witness, and knew no better way than to go personally to all the ships in ordinary, until the individual was found. He actually visited every sea-port town, and boarded every ship, till in the very *last* port and on the very *last* ship which remained, the individual was found, and found to be possessed of just the facts and information which were necessary. By the labors of Clarkson and his cotemporaries an incredible excitement was produced throughout all England. The pictures and models of slave ships, accounts of the cruelties practised in the trade, were circulated with an industry which left not a man, woman, or child in England uninstructed. In disseminating information, and in awakening feeling and conscience, the women of England were particularly earnest, and labored with that whole-hearted devotion which characterizes the sex.

It seems that after the committee had published the facts, and sent them to every town in England, Clarkson followed them up by journeying to all the places, to see that they were read and attended to. Of the state of feeling at this time, Clarkson gives the following account:

"And first I may observe, that there was no town through which I passed, in which there was not some one individual who had left off the use of sugar. In the smaller towns there were from ten to fifty, by estimation, and in the larger, from two to five hundred, who made this sacrifice to virtue. These were of all ranks and parties. Rich and poor, churchmen and dissenters had adopted the measure. Even grocers had left off trading in the article in some places. In gentlemen's families, where the master had set the example, the servants had often voluntarily followed it; and even children, who were capable of understanding the history of the sufferings of the Africans, excluded with the most virtuous resolution the sweets, to which they had been accustomed, from their lips. By the best computation I was able to make, from notes taken down in my journey, no fewer than three hundred thousand persons had abandoned the use of sugar." It was the reality, depth, and earnestness of the public feeling, thus aroused, which pressed with resistless force upon the government; for the government of England yields to popular demands, quite as readily as that of America.

After years of protracted struggle, the victory was at last won. The slave-trade was finally abolished through all the British empire; and not only so, but the English nation committed, with the whole force of its national influence, to seek the abolition of the slave-trade in all the nations of the earth. But the wave of feeling did not rest there; the investigations had brought before the English conscience the horrors and abominations of slavery itself, and the agitation never ceased till slavery was finally abolished through all the British provinces. At this time the religious mind and conscience of England gained, through this very struggle, a power which it never has lost. The principle adopted by them was the same so sublimely adopted by the church in America, in reference to the Foreign Missionary cause: "The field is the world." They saw and felt that as the example and practice of England had been powerful in giving sanction to this evil, and particularly in introducing it into America, that there was the greatest reason why she should never intermit her efforts till the wrong was righted throughout the earth.

Clarkson to his last day never ceased to be interested in the subject, and took the warmest interest in all movements for the abolition of slavery in America.

One of his friends, during my visit at this place, read me a manuscript letter from him, written at a very advanced age, in which he speaks with the utmost ardor and enthusiasm of the first anti-slavery movements of Cassius Clay in Kentucky. The same friend described him to me as a cheerful, companionable being,—frank and simple-hearted, and with a good deal of quiet humor.

It is remarkable of him that with such intense feeling for human suffering as he had, and worn down and exhausted as he was, by the dreadful miseries and sorrows with which he was constantly obliged to be familiar, he never yielded to a spirit of bitterness or denunciation.

The narrative which he gives is as calm and unimpassioned, and as free from any trait of this kind, as the narrative of the evangelist.

I have given this sketch of what Clarkson did, that you may better appreciate the feelings with which I visited the place.

The old stone house, the moat, the draw-bridge, all spoke of days of violence long gone by, when no man was safe except within fortified walls, and every man's house literally had to be his castle.

To me it was interesting as the dwelling of a conqueror, as one who had not wrestled with flesh and blood merely, but with principalities and powers, and the rulers of the darkness of this world, and who had overcome, as his great Master did before him, by faith, and prayer, and labor.

We were received with much cordiality by the widow of Clarkson, now in her eighty-fourth year. She has been a woman of great energy and vigor, and an efficient co-laborer in his plans of benevolence.

She is now quite feeble. I was placed under the care of a respectable female servant, who forthwith installed me in a large chamber overlooking the court-yard, which had been Clarkson's own room; the room where for years, many of his most important labors had been conducted, and from whence his soul had ascended to the reward of the just.

The servant who attended me seemed to be quite a superior woman; like many of the servants in respectable English families. She had grown up in the family, and was identified with it; its ruling aims and purposes had become hers. She had been the personal attendant of Clarkson, and his nurse during his last sickness; she had evidently understood, and been interested in his plans, and the veneration with which she therefore spoke of him, had the sanction of intelligent appreciation.

A daughter of Clarkson, who was married to a neighboring clergyman, with her husband, was also present on this day.

After dinner we rode out to see the old church, in whose enclosure the remains of Clarkson repose. It was just such a still, quiet, mossy old church, as you have read of in story-books, with the grave-yard spread all around it, like a thoughtful mother, who watches the resting of her children.

The grass in the yard was long and green, and the daisy, which in other places lies like a little button on the ground, here had a richer fringe of crimson, and a stalk about six inches high. It is, I well know, the vital influence from the slumbering dust beneath, which gives the richness to this grass and these flowers; but let not that be a painful thought; let it rather cheer us, that beauty should spring from ashes, and life smile brighter from the near presence of death. The grave of Clarkson was near the church, enclosed by a railing and marked by a simple white marble slab; it was carefully tended and planted with flowers. In the church was an old book of records, and among other curious inscriptions, was one recording how a pious committee of old Noll's army had been there, knocking off saints' noses, and otherwise purging the church from the relics of idolatry.

Near by the church was the parsonage, the home of my friends, a neat, pleasant, sequestered dwelling, of about the style of a New England country parsonage.

The effect of the whole together was inexpressibly beautiful to me. For a wonder, it was a pleasant day, and this is a thing always to be thankfully acknowledged in England. The calm stillness of the afternoon, the seclusion of the whole place, the silence only broken by the cawing of the rooks, the ancient church, the mossy graves with their flowers and green grass, the sunshine and the tree shadows, all seemed to mingle together in a kind of hazy dream of peacefulness and rest. How natural it is to say of some place sheltered, simple, cool, and retired, here one might find peace, as if peace came from without, and not from within. In the shadiest and stillest places may be the most turbulent hearts, and there are hearts which, through the busiest scenes, carry with them unchanging peace. As we were walking back, we passed many cottages of the poor.

I noticed, with particular pleasure, the invariable flower garden attached to each. Some pansies in one of them attracted my attention by their peculiar beauty, so very large and richly colored. On being introduced to the owner of them, she, with cheerful alacrity, offered me some of the finest. I do not doubt of there being suffering and misery in the agricultural population of England, but still there are multitudes of cottages, which are really very pleasant objects, as were all these. The cottagers had that bright, rosy look of health which we seldom see in America, and appeared to be both polite and self-respecting.

In the evening we had quite a gathering of friends from the neighborhood—intelligent, sensible, earnest, people—who had grown up in the love of the anti-slavery cause as into religion. The subject of conversation was: "The duty of English people to free themselves from any participation in American slavery, by taking means to encourage the production of free cotton in the British provinces."

It is no more impossible or improbable that something effective may be done in this way, than that the slave-trade should have been abolished. Every great movement seems an impossibility at first. There is no end to the number of things declared and proved impossible, which have been done already, so that this may do something yet.

Mrs. Clarkson had retired from the room early; after a while she sent for me to her sitting-room. The faithful attendant of whom I spoke was with her. She wished to show me some relics of her husband, his watch and seals, some of his papers and manuscripts; among these was the identical prize essay with which he began his career, and a commentary on the Gospels, which he had written with great care, for the use of his grandson. His seal attracted my attention—it was that kneeling figure, of the negro, with clasped hands, which was at first adopted as the badge of the cause, when every means was being made use of to arouse the public mind and keep the subject before the attention. Mr. Wedgewood, the celebrated procelain manufacturer, designed a cameo, with this representation, which was much worn as an ornament by ladies. It was engraved on the seal of the Anti-Slavery Society, and was used by its members in sealing all their letters. This of Clarkson's was handsomely engraved on a large, old-fashioned cornelian, and surely if we look with emotion on the sword of a departed hero, which, at best, we can consider only as a necessary evil, we may look with unmingled pleasure on this memorial of a bloodless victory.

When I retired to my room for the night I could not but feel that the place was hallowed—unceasing prayer had there been offered for the enslaved and wronged race of Africa by that noble and brotherly heart. I could not but feel that that those prayers had had a wider reach than the mere extinction of slavery in one land or country, and that their benign influence would not cease till not a slave was left upon the face of the earth.

H. B. Stowe.

Teaching the Slave to Read.

MUCH has been discussed and written, both at the North and South, concerning the policy and propriety of permitting those in bondage to gain the rudiments of a common education.

Many who *conscientiously* (for having lived among them, I do believe that there *are* "conscientious" slave-owners) hold their laborers in servitude, believe that the experiment might be successfully tried. Indeed, it is often tried on plantations, even in States where the law enforces strict penalties against it. They believe that the slaves, if permitted to learn to read, would be more moral, faithful and obedient; and they cannot reconcile it with their sense of duty to keep from them the perusal of the Bible.

The majority, however, think differently; and the majority will always make the laws. *They* believe that there is a talismanic power in even the alphabet of knowledge, to arouse in the bondsman powers which they would crush for ever. They believe that one truth leads on to another, and that the mind, once aroused to inquiry, will never rest until it has found out its native independence of man's dominion. They point triumphantly, in proof of the policy of their system, to the "spoiled slave," as they term many of those in whose training the opposite course has been pursued. More trouble, vexation, and insubordination, they confidently allege, has been caused by permitting slaves to learn to read, than by any other indulgence.

It may be so; it is certain that, in many instances, masters have failed to win the gratitude to which they thought themselves justly entitled, for their kindness and care. They have found their servants growing discontented and idle, where they hoped to make them docile and happy. Searching for the cause of this, they perhaps turn upon the course of training they have followed, and accuse it of being opposed to the best interests of the slave. Could such reasoners but look upon the matter in its true perspective, they would cease to wonder that "good" should, in their view, "work out evil." *Learning* and *Slavery* can never compromise; they are as the antagonistic poles of the magnet.

In the first place, Slavery blunts the mind, and renders it, in its early years, unsusceptible to those impressions which are generally so lasting, when made upon youthful minds. Many who have tried to educate colored children, have been led to accuse *the race* of natural inferiority in its capacity to gain knowledge. We have no right to draw *that* inference from the few attempts which have been made on a part of the race whose mental faculties have, through many generations, been crippled by disuse.

I had once under my charge, for a short time, a negro girl, born in Africa—"Margru" of the "Armistad," with whose history most are familiar. On *her* ancestory hung no clog of depression, except that of native wildness. There was no lack of aptitude to learn in her case. She astonished all by the ease with which she acquired knowledge, particularly in mathematical science. That a native heathen should be a better recipient of knowledge than one brought up in the midst of American civilization, speaks well for "the race," but ill for "the system," which has trained the latter.

Not only is this native dulness to be overcome, but *time* for study is to be found—time enough for the faculties to unbend from the pressure of labor, and fix themselves upon the mental task. This is what few employers consider themselves able to afford. Once a week, in their opinion, is quite often enough for the slave to repeat his lesson; and through the week he may forget it. No wonder that both the indulgent master and the teacher—yes, and the learner, too, often become discouraged, and give up the task before the Word of God is unlocked to "the poor," for whom it was expressly written!

I speak as one who has *felt* these obstacles, having, with the approval of one of the class to whom I have alluded, taken charge of a Sunday school among his servants. More attentive and grateful pupils I never had, but it has pained my heart to feel the difficulty of leading them even to the *threshold* of knowledge; and there leaveing them!

In an adjoining household, however, it was still worse. George, a light-colored "boy" of twenty-five, the "factotum" of his mistress, was the husband of our cook, Letty. I had succeeded in taking Letty through several chapters in the New Testament, and this had aroused the ambition of George.

"What do you think?" exclaimed one of the family to me, one morning; "Mrs. —— has been *whipping* George!"

"Why! for what could that have been? I thought he was a favorite servant!"

"For taking lessons of Letty in the spelling-book!"

It was even so. The poor fellow wanted to learn to stammer in his Testament, and Letty, like any true-hearted wife, had given him the little assistance she could render. The whipping failed of its intended effect, however. Going one evening, at a late hour, into Letty's cabin, I found George seated by her on the floor, in the corner of their mud fire-place, poring intently over the forbidden spelling-book! He started up confused, but seeing who it was, he was reassured, and went on with his lesson! Whether George, Letty, or any of those who have gained the rudiments of science, will be *more happy* in their servitude, is to me exceedingly doubtful. Thus far the severer classes of masters have the right; a slave, to be perfectly contented *as* a slave, must be in total ignorance. But better, far better, greater suffering, if it bring enlargement of man's higher being, than that system that would *smother* the soul in its bodily case. Let the slave have the key to the gate of Life Eternal, even if his pathway through this life must be more thickly sown with thorns. Let the opposing principles wage, until the right of *one* is asserted. And, oh! above all pray for the day when these fetters shall be stricken from the souls God has created, wherewith to people, we firmly trust, no mean "tabernacle" of His New Jerusalem!

Mary Irving

THIBODAUX, NOV. 25, 1853.

"It is a good book, and will be read by thousands."—*Chicago Journal.*

"Some of Mr. Willis' happiest hits and most graceful specimens of compositions are here included."—*N. Y. Evangelist.*

"Fresh, lively, gay, and gossipping, these 'Fun Jottings' deservedly merit the enduring garb in which they appear."—*Home Gazette.*

"One of Willis' pleasant books, in which the reader is always sure to find entertainment."—*Philadelphia Mirror.*

"The contents are better than the title."—*N. Y. Tribune.*

"A volume of light sketches, written in Mr. Willis' most amusing style, and will be read by everybody."—*Detroit Advertiser.*

"It contains the best specimen of the prose writings of Mr. Willis."—*Montgomery Gazette.*

"The book is entertaining and spicy—just the kind of reading to keep one 'wide awake' during the long nights that are now approaching."—*Phil. News.*

"For laughter without folly, for a specific in innocent mirthfulness against *ennui* and *hypo*—as a cordial to the animal spirits when drooping with care or flagging with excess of labor—this volume of 'Fun-Jottings' bears the palm."—*N. Y. Independent.*

"It is funny and fascinating—a collection of Willis' dashing sketches—half comic, half pathetic."—*Cincinnati Herald.*

"Mr. Willis' reputation as a story writer, has long been well established, and lovers of this kind of reading will find a rich entertainment in this volume."—*Hartford Times.*

THE FARM AND THE FIRESIDE;

OR,

THE ROMANCE OF AGRICULTURE,

BEING

HALF HOURS OF LIFE IN THE COUNTRY, FOR RAINY DAYS AND WINTER EVENINGS.

BY REV. JOHN L. BLAKE, D.D.

AUTHOR OF FARMER'S EVERY-DAY BOOK; THE FARMER AT HOME; AND A GENERAL BIOGRAPHICAL DICTIONARY.

COMMENDATIONS OF THE PERIODICAL PRESS.

From the Ohio Farmer.

DR. BLAKE is justly regarded as one of the best agricultural writers in the country, and the work before us is one of the most interesting productions of his pen. Its peculiar merit, as a work for the fireside, consists in the variety of its topics, its plain and simple, yet attractive style, its fine engravings, and the interesting romance which the author has thrown around Rural and Agricultural Life. In this respect, "The Farm and the Fireside" is a work well adapted to the youthful mind. We hope it may be extensively read, as it cannot fail to improve the taste and promote inquiry in the most useful and practical of all departments of science.

From the New-York Evangelist.

The aim of the author has been to throw over labor, home and agricultural life, their true dignity and charm; to introduce the farmer to the delights and privileges of his lot; to embellish the cares of toil with those kindly sentiments so naturally associated with the country and its employments. It is a pleasant book—one that will enliven the fireside, elevate and purify the thoughts, and, at the same time, impart a great deal of valuable agricultural knowledge. We know not how the natural trains of thought of the farmer could be more aptly met or more safely and agreeably led, than they are by these brief and varied discussions. The range is as wide as life itself—morals, religion business, recreation, education, home, wife and daughters—every relation and duty is touched upon, genially and instinctively.

From the New-York Tribune.

We have here another highly instructive and entertaining volume from an author, who had laid the community under large obligations by the enterprise and tact with which he has so frequently catered to the popular taste for descriptions of rural life. Its contents are of a very miscellaneous character, embracing sketches of natural history, accounts of successful farming operations, anecdotes of distinguished characters, singular personal reminiscences, pithy moral reflections, and numerous picturesof household life in the country. No family can add this volume to their collection of books without increasing their sources of pleasure and profit.

From the Northern Christian Advocate.

The venerable author of this work is entitled to the warmest thanks of the public for his numerous and valuable contributions to our literature. He is truly an American classic. We have been conversant with his writings for the last twenty years, and have always found them both useful and entertaining in a high degree. His writings on Agriculture contain much real science, with numerous illustrative incidents, anecdotes, and aphorisms, all in the most lively and pleasing manner. By this means the dry details of farming business are made to possess all the interest of romance. The style is clear, easy, and dignified; the matter instructive, philosophical, and persuasive. This work is an eloquent plea for the noble and independent pursuit of Agriculture.

From the National Magazine.

We return our thanks for the new volume of Dr. Blake, "The Farm and the Fireside, or the Romance of Agriculture, being Half Hours and

Sketches of Life in the Country," a charming title, certainly, and one that smacks of the man as well as of the country. Eschewing the dryness of scientific forms and erudite details, the author presents detached, but most entertaining, and often very suggestive articles on a great variety of topics—from the "Wild Goose" to "Conscience in the Cow,"—from the "Value of Lawyers in a Community" to the "Objections to early Marriages." The book is, in fine, quite unique, and just such a one as the farmer would like to pore over at his fireside on long winter evenings.

From the New-York Recorder.

"The Farm and the Fireside," is a most interesting and valuable work, being a series of Sketches relating to Agriculture and the numerous kindred arts and sciences, interspersed with miscellaneous moral instruction, adapted to the life of the farmer.

From the Germantown Telegraph.

We have looked through this work and read some of the "Sketches," and feel a degree of satisfaction in saying that it possesses decided merit, and will commend itself, wherever known, as a volume of much social interest and entertainment. The sketches comprise "Country Life" generally—some of them are just sufficiently touched with romance to give them additional zest; while others are purely practical, and relate to the farmer's pursuit. We regard it as a valuable book, and are sorry our limits will not admit of bestowing upon it such a notice as it really deserves.

From Harper's New Monthly Magazine.

This work is a collection of miscellaneous sketches on the Romance of Agriculture and Rural Life. Matters of fact, however, are not excluded from the volume, which is well adapted for reading in the snatches of leisure enjoyed at the farmer's fireside.

From the True Democrat.

Dr. Blake's publications are all of a high order, and are doing a most important work towards refining the taste, improving the intellect, and rendering attractive the various branches of Agricultural science. Indeed we know no author who has so successfully blended the romantic, the rural and beautiful with the poetical, the useful, and true, as has Dr. Blake. This is a peculiar feature of all his works. His style is plain, simple, and perspicuous; and, with unusual tact and judgment, he so manages to insinuate himself upon you, that you are at once amused, delighted, and instructed with the subject he is discussing. In this respect he relieves the study of agricultural science from the abstruseness of technical science, and thus renders himself easily comprehended by all classes of readers.

From the New-York Evening Post.

The author's object is to improve the soil through the mind—not so much to place in the hands of farmers the best methods of raising large crops—for these he refers them to Leibig's Agricultural Chemistry, and to treatises of the like description—but to make them feel how useful, agreeable, and ennobling, is the profession of agriculture, and, above all, how profitable the business must become when skilfully and economically carried on. These money-making considerations are, we suspect, the best moral guano that can be applied to the farmer's spiritual soil. The author writes well of the countryman's independence, the good effect of fresh salubrious air upon his health, and the moral influence of his every-day intimacy with nature upon his mind.

"The Farm and the Fireside" is a kind of Bucolical annual—to be read in seasons of leisure—intended for the Phyllises and Chloes, as well as for the Strephons and Lindors. Dr. Blake has enriched it with curious anecdotes of domestic animals, and of the best way of raising and selling them. He describes model-farms, and the large incomes made from them. He expatiates on the advantages of matrimony in rural life, expounds the true theory of choosing a helpmate, discusses the advantages of Sunday-Schools, and recommends neatness of attire and punctuality in bathing. In short, this volume is as diversified in its aspect as the small garden of a judicious cultivator, where, in a limited space, useful cabbages, potatoes, and all the solid esculent greens, grow side by side with choice fruits and pleasant flowers.

The contents of the work are of the first order and unexceptionable.—*Rochester Daily Union.*

The story is not only well written, but it has merits in the dramatic grouping of incidents, graphic delineation of character, and the affecting interest which attracts and supports the reader's attention through the whole work, from the opening scene to the finale.—*Rochester Daily Democrat.*

This is a new work from the pen of the gifted author of the "Silver Lake Stories." It is got up in a style of mechanical elegance equal to the issues of Putnam and Appleton, and the quality of its contents will not be found behind that of three-fourths of the publications that emanate from the pens of more wide-known authors, and from publishing houses that employ none but the *best writers.*—*Canandaigua Messenger.*

It is a story designed to illustrate the deplorable effects of a neglect of proper parental discipline in infancy; in a well-written preface, the authoress, "Cousin Cicely," assures us it is substantially a narrative of facts. It traces the career of a spoiled and petted boy, whose mother was too weak and indolent to restrain him as she ought, through the several stages of a perverse childhood, a reckless boyhood, and a passionate, ungovernable youth, till this victim of a parent's folly is found in a felon's cell, with the mark of Cain on his brow.—*Auburn Daily Advertiser.*

The authoress, who, by the way, need not be afraid to sail under her own proper colors hereafter, claims that most of the incidents are taken from real life; a very creditable averment, as the work, with slight modifications in each individual case, would prove a faithful portraiture of the early training and subsequent career of nine-tenths of the victims of the gallows, and of the penitentiary.—*Mirror, Lyons, N. Y.*

The writer of this, and of many other pleasant volumes—"Cousin Cicely," as she chooses to be called—is gifted with rare talents, which she is wisely devoting to useful ends. Her charming "Silver Lake Stories," have effected much good, and this work is well calculated to do the same, both with children of the larger and of the smaller growth. * * * Difficulties of various natures arise, on the last and most important of which hangs the catastrophe of the story. But what that is, and how the book ends, is for the reader to find out, not for us to tell.—*Albany Eve Journal.*

* * * One of the domestic sort—speaking of home, dwelling upon home affections and family character, and the incidents of common life, yet as deeply interesting as the most romantic narrative. It has not been paraded before the public with ostentatious praise; but it will be far more acceptable to the reader than many works that have thus attracted interest in advance, without being able to meet and repay it.—*Albany Atlas.*

www.ingramcontent.com/pod-product-compliance
Lightning Source LLC
LaVergne TN
LVHW010206110826
845151LV00002B/620